Sparkfor

To Pam and Terry,

with my very best wishes

Jeff Clew

8.3.91

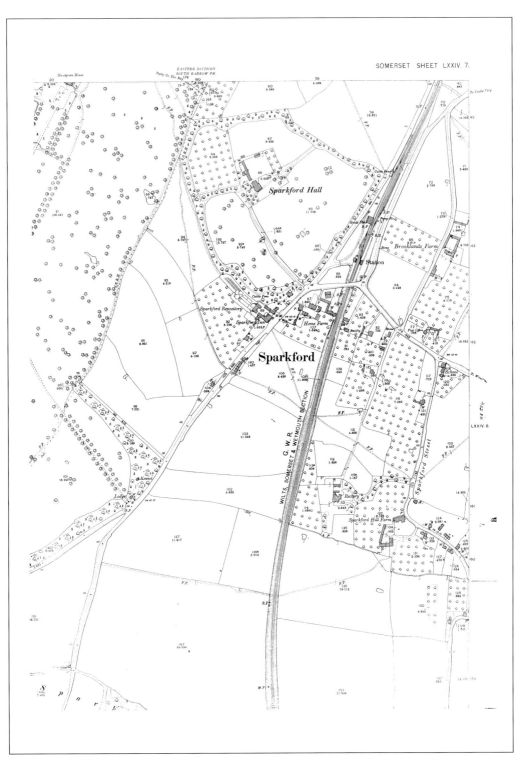

Frontispiece: Sparkford, reproduced from the 1903 Ordnance Survey map.

Sparkford

MEMORIES OF THE PAST

Jeff Clew

To Audrey, Alison and Philippa

First published in 1997.

British Library Cataloguing-in-Publication Data:
A catalogue record for this book is available from the British Library.

ISBN 1 85960 009 3

Haynes Publishing, Sparkford, Nr Yeovil, Somerset BA22 7JJ.

Typeset by J. H. Haynes & Co. Ltd.

Printed in Great Britain.

Front cover illustration: *Sparkford church in early spring.* (Mrs M. Raynor)

As part of our ongoing market research, we are always pleased to receive comments about our books, suggestions for new titles, or requests for catalogues. Please write to: The Editorial Director, Haynes Publishing, Sparkford, Nr Yeovil, Somerset, BA22 7JJ.

Contents

Foreword

It is said that from each disaster some good must come. When Jeff Clew broke his foot last year it was a disaster for him, but what a good thing it proved to be. It provided him with the incentive to compile this history of our village.

To have a book about Sparkford is a grand idea. I am conscious that we have already lost many of our older parishioners, who have taken with them their knowledge and vivid recollections of the past.

I know that this book, which contains many old photographs, personal memories, and accounts of past events, will be of great interest to us all. It will surely become a very useful source of reference.

Fred Warren
Chairman: Sparkford Parish Council
November 1996

Introduction

Sparkford is a small village, described in old records as being a Parish in the Hundred of Catsash. Its population has grown from 239 in 1801 to the present level of some 500 inhabitants, and it now lies mostly to the south of the old London to Exeter road (A303) which has been bypassed in recent years. Many who travel to the West Country whilst on their way to Devon and Cornwall for their holidays will know it as a pleasant and convenient place to stop for lunch. The village lies about 7 miles from Wincanton and is just over 50 miles from the City of Exeter. It is situated by the River Cam, close to the site of Camelot, of Arthurian legend.

Sparkford from the air, before the bypass was built, showing the Sparkford Inn in the centre foreground with the sheep sheds for the cattle market at its rear. Home Farm is on the right with some of the farm buildings and the Hare's Nest almost hidden by the trees.

Another aerial view of Sparkford taken at the same time as the previous illustration, showing the High Street and the A359 leading to Castle Cary. The railway line is readily evident and in the background the sawmills site can be seen in the fork between the railway and the road.

It may be wondered why I, as a relatively recent inhabitant who moved into the Parish with my family during late 1978, should have written this book. The reason is quite simple. As Editor of *The Parish News* I was becoming only too aware that we were losing many of our older residents who were born and bred in Sparkford. Sadly, they took with them so many memories of the past that no longer can be recaptured. Old photographs were becoming a problem too. Even if most of them were uncaptioned so that one had to rely on the memory of others to recall to what they related or the names of various individuals, they were only too often destroyed by well-meaning relatives who had not realised their true value. Someone had to come to the rescue before it was too late. In a sense I feel a small part of the story, as for the last few years before my retirement I had my office in Home Farm, the former home of John Perry and his family. Furthermore, by coincidence my wife Audrey was evacuated to Sparkford during part of World War 2 so that, if anything, she knew more about the village than I did myself.

I have derived a great deal of enjoyment in putting this book together. I seemed at first to start out with a huge number of pieces of a jigsaw that looked as though they were unrelated, especially as I was unfamiliar with the names of many individuals or the names of houses and areas of land. Thanks to the help of so many, the pieces soon began to fit together until a complete story emerged.

I have tried my best to check and double-check the details I have been given and I can only apologise if errors appear here and there, largely as a result of fading memories. Hopefully, I have not overlooked in the list of acknowledgements and references given at the end of this book any of those who so kindly volunteered to provide either information or photographs. They welcomed me into their homes and so willingly gave up their time to talk about bygone days.

Virtually all of the photographs are copies and bore no reference to the origin of the photographer. If I have inadvertently transgressed anyone's copyright I can only apologise. Some photographs have deteriorated from storage but I have used them because they provide precious glimpses of the past that were not obtainable elsewhere. I am especially grateful to those who helped caption them even if it was often the case of making an inspired guess. If any caption contains errors or seems inadequate, I would be greatly obliged if anyone can provide some of the missing information or put a name to any person not listed.

I am especially indebted to the Rev. Guy Bennett, the Rector of Oxted, who not only provided the relevant extracts of the Bennett family history compiled by his brother, but also visited me with the complete copy so that I could see for the first time what Henry Bennett and his wife Emily actually looked like. The Bennett family formed the core of the story during the 19th century as owners and benefactors of most of the village properties until the latter were put up for auction in December 1918. Further useful information came in the form of a handwritten book compiled by Edith Mary Bennett (1869-1946), which was kindly lent to me by Mrs Diana Gordon Clark.

I must also mention David Wood who, though terminally ill, so kindly provided the answers to many of my questions about village life and lent me his press cuttings book as well as his photograph collection. Sadly, he died as I was putting the finishing touches to this manuscript. I would dearly have liked him to see the finished book.

This book is quite different from any I have written before. I can only hope it will match up to expectations, especially those to whom Sparkford has always been their home. I am aware there may have been a few others I should have visited, but the amount of time at my disposal was never as much as I would have liked. This also applies to those who could have made additional contributions had I known of their existence or whereabouts. To all of them I offer my sincere apologies and hope they will understand; the need to complete my manuscript to a tight deadline was always the over-riding factor.

My grateful thanks to Helen Tracy who proof read the manuscript and also ensured its grammatical correctness and freedom from typographicals. I must also thank Jim Windsor for checking the content to make sure it is as factually correct as possible, Tilzey Studios of Yeovil for making an excellent job of copying the old photographs, and John Haynes O.B.E. for offering to publish this book. It is appropriate that he should have done so as yet another extension to his much appreciated service to the community.

Jeff Clew
Sparkford
January 1997

Sparkford Through the Ages

Despite its small size, Sparkford is mentioned in the Domesday Book, using its old spelling of Spercheforde and listed as the land of Walter de Dowai. The entry states that *Fulchin holds of Walter Spercheforde. Eluuacre held it in the time of King Edward , and gelded* (taxes paid to the Crown by land owners) *for five hides* (a measure of land) *and one virgate* (a quarter of a hide or 30 acres) *of land. In demense* (land held and possessed by the owner himself) *are two carcuates and a half* (as much land as could be tilled by one plough and eight oxen in a year) *and six servants, and nine villanes*, and seven cottagers with four ploughs. There is a mill of seven shillings and sixpence rent, and forty acres of meadow, and one furlong of wood in length* (the length of a furrow, 220 yards) *and breadth. It is worth four pounds, now one hundred shillings.* (*A villane in feudal England meant any member of a class of serfs and peasants who, by the 13th century, had become freemen in their legal relations to all others except their lords, to whom they remained subject as slaves).

John Collinson's *History of Somerset* dated 1791 traces the parish's connection with various families, claiming that at an early date it formed part of the great barony of the Lovels, lords of Castle Cary. Ralph de Sparkeforde, named after the village, held one knight's fee there of Henry Lovel and his descendants long continued as tenants under the successive possessors of this lordship. Sparkford was, however, at some time held by the Burnell family, of whom Robert Burnell was Bishop of Bath and Wells at the time of King Edward I. After them came the Handlos' and the Rogers', successive mesne lords. The Lovels however were lords paramount and from them the ownership of Sparkford descended in the same manner as Castle Cary to the Seymours, the Lords Zouche of Harringworth, and Willoughby Lord Broke, at length to be purchased by Richard Newman, whose descendant, Francis Newman of North Cadbury, was present holder at the time of Collinson's book.

ANN BLANDFORD'S CHARITY

Ann Blandford, who lived in the village and died in 1767, left the Parish £7 in her will. She proposed that the annual interest should be applied to the 'second' poor and be administered by the local clergy. Eventually, the principal sum was lost sight of, although it was secured in the Parish Rates and seven shillings was paid annually by the Churchwardens. A change in the arrangement was made from 1819-1837 when seven shillings was raised out of the poor rates and invested in a savings bank in the name of the Minister of the Parish. He dispensed its interest in the form of linen, bread or fuel as he thought fit, to the needy.

SPARKFORD'S HOUSING AND POPULATION

The village originally lay mostly to the south of the church, around a field known as Lickhill, bordered by the River Cam. It is said that when the Russians (?) came to Sparkford they stood on Sparkford Hill, whilst the English gathered on Cadbury Castle. In the resulting battle the English licked the Russians, hence the name Lickhill. True or otherwise, skeletons of indeterminate age, arranged in regular rows, were unearthed before being re-interred on Sparkford Hill near the old lime kiln. A ghostly funeral is alleged to have been seen along Lickhill Knap, the slight incline running up from the river, presumably making its way to the church. Another regular sighting occurred close to the old lime kiln, preceded by the ghostly footsteps of a man dragging a foot.

In 1791 there were 41 houses, of which 27 were near to the church, the remainder being along the turnpike road. The total number of residents was 230. According to C. & J. Greenwood's *Somerset Delineated* of 1822, the number of inhabited houses at its time of publication had risen to 37, and of the 52 families, 40 were employed in agricultural work. By 1831 the number of inhabited houses had dwindled to 25.

The turnpike road was owned by the Langport, Somerton and Castle Cary Trust, dissolved in 1879. Evidence of a turnpike gate in the village was found a good many years later by William Pittard, the village blacksmith at that time. He unearthed what appeared to be the massive wooden base of a huge gatepost on which a toll gate would have hung.

THE BENNETTS OF SPARKFORD

Sparkford Hall was destined to become the focal point of the village after its construction was completed around 1848. Its first occupant was the elderly mother of Henry Bennett, but when she died in 1853, Henry and his family took up residence. A very colourful character, who was both the village Squire and its Parson and left his mark in the village in no small way, it seems appropriate that something should be known about him and his elder son who succeeded him. It was not until Henry Bennett became Lord of the Manor that Sparkford had a resident squire.

HENRY BENNETT B.C.L., J.P., – SQUIRE AND PARSON

Henry Bennett, born on 30th October 1795, was the youngest and favourite son of James Bennett, of Cadbury Court. Cadbury Court was the baronial residence of the ancient Lords of Cadbury, built by Sir Henry Hastings, the third Earl of Huntingdon in 1572. It became the residence of the Bennett family much later and when James

Bennett died in 1815, Henry inherited Sparkford village at the age of 19. Sadly, the division of the estate had made it unworkable economically. This and Henry's lavish Continental tours, which he had undertaken to offset his disappointment in not being allowed to join the Army, led to the eventual decline in the family fortunes.

It was during his travels that Henry met Emily Moberly, the daughter of an English merchant resident in St Petersburg. His courtship led to a proposal of marriage and they were married in that city on 20th July 1821. Edward Moberly, Emily's father, was the British Consul and had not been happy about the proposed union as he considered his future son-in-law should have a profession. As a result, Henry had returned to England on 29th July 1820 to be re-admitted to Trinity College, Cambridge where, in 1822, he obtained a First Class Honours Degree as a Batchelor of Law. Emily considered the Church would be preferable to any other profession and that she would be happy to be a clergyman's wife. Henry concurred and they married in St Petersburg whilst he was still studying at Cambridge. Their wishes were fulfilled when, on 14th July 1822, Henry was ordained Deacon by the Bishop of Gloucester and went as curate to Sidmouth, Devon. Their first child, Henry Edward, was born there in September 1822. Subsequently, Henry was ordained priest by the Bishop of Chester in 1823.

He took up the family livings of South Cadbury and Sparkford in 1831 and 1836 respectively, taking residence in Hazlegrove House initially, having informed the Bishop there was no house in either parish fit for a gentleman. Although two daughters were born whilst they were at Hazlegrove House, Emily in 1823 and Julia in June 1825, the Bennetts with their three children returned to see the Moberlys in St Petersburg during 1826. The visit coincided with another Continental tour and it was whilst they were in Genoa that Edward James was born in March 1829. In Naples, where Harry again acted as English chaplain, two more children were born, Mary Isobel in February 1831 and George in August 1832. It was not until the autumn of 1833 that they arrived back in England after the Bishop had demanded that Henry must return to his parishes or resign.

After staying for a short while in Bath, whilst Sparkford Hall was being built, they moved to Woolston House, where a son was born who died soon after. They then moved to South Cadbury Rectory, where another son, James Arthur, was born in 1835, later to become Rector of the parish. Two more girls, Elisabeth Mary and Susan Fanny, were also born there. According to Phelp's *History of Somerset, Vol. 11 (p.405)*, the aisle of South Cadbury church was fitted with private pews and the nave with open seats, some having carving on their ends. On one was inscribed 'Henry Bennett 1835'.

In 1841 Sparkford Hall had still to be completed, so Henry and his family settled at Sparkford Rectory. He had been appointed Rector of Sparkford in 1836. Mostly of Henry's construction, it occupied the site and inherited the back parts of an older building. Agnes Emily was born there in 1841 and Charles William three years later. He was the last of the family, destined to become a future Rector of Sparkford.

Sparkford Hall in more recent years, after the Bennett family had left and it had been sold in the village auction of December 1918.

Sparkford Hall was finally completed around 1848. Henry's mother, who had always shown an interest in the house, was the first to take up residence. She had struck a bargain with Henry whereby if she was allowed to remain at Sparkford Hall until her death, she would furnish it with furniture from Cadbury Court. When she died in 1853, the Bennetts made their final move and leased the Rectory.

Constructed of Ham Hill stone, the symetrical design of the Hall is supposed to be based on that of an Italian villa. At the back of the house is a stone that bears the date 1828, probably the date on which building commenced. The marble mantelpiece in the drawing room, which was later displaced, had been made originally for Apsley House. However, it did not fit and the Duke of Wellington gave orders for it to be sold. It was subsequently purchased by Henry Bennett.

In his dual capacity of Squire and Parson it is alleged Henry ruled Sparkford fairly but somewhat strictly. Every house in the village was in his possession and no Nonconformist was allowed to reside there. Nor was he kindly disposed towards Methodists, who had to build their chapel at West Camel. He would not allow any illegitimate child to be born in the parish either, with the result that local girls whose children would be born out of wedlock used to travel to Queen Camel for their confinement.

Henry rebuilt almost all the cottages in Sparkford, to create what could, in its day, be regarded as a model village. Much to the concern of the surrounding squirearchy, he also opened a school and paid a 'dame' to teach in it, in a house opposite Manor Farm. The south porch at Sparkford Church he enlarged and converted into the Hall pews, and being a rather generously proportioned man in his old age, he had a shallow alcove scraped at the back of the pulpit to accommodate him more comfortably. He used to preach in a long, black gown and in later years took his luncheon with him so that he could eat it in the vestry before Evensong, the best Sunday School scholar being given what remained!

A keen rider to hounds, it is said that following a parishioner's complaint to the Bishop, Henry was obliged to cease taking services with his horse hitched to the church gate and with his surplice over his hunting gear! He disliked a quiet horse and always carried with him a great whip when driving with his wife sitting beside him on the box seat. His horse often bolted, when he would say to his wife "Take off my hat", which she would then hold for him, whilst he took command. He was renowned for his accidents, especially around Blackford and Cadbury Hills.

Living in an area that abounded with alleged hauntings he also had a great reputation as a layer of ghosts, and was sent for whenever the occasion arose. At that time there was still a considerable belief in witchcraft and the supernatural in Sparkford, but as the Squire would not like it, the belief was never openly voiced. Many were even reluctant to talk about such things to others as they thought it would make them look silly.

A lover of buildings, the old Scottish gardener at Hazlegrove House once said of him "See the artistic talent in Sparkford; no two cottages alike and the boulevards". The latter comprised an avenue of limes from the bridge to the school and oaks to the gate of Hazlegrove. Henry was also devoted to planting and to beautiful trees. It is said he always carried laurel seeds in his pocket for laurel grew in abundance all about his houses. At the Hall, between the wall and the porch, he also planted a pomegranate, which sadly never flowered until the year after his death.

He and Mrs Bennett used to go to church each Sunday in their bath chairs, side by side, whilst the cottagers stood at their doors to salute them. When at one time he encountered an agitator haranguing a small group, he remarked as he passed that "It would be quite lawful to duck that man in the river". The group showed such willingness to do so that the speaker fled! It is alleged it was Henry's practice to visit on a Monday any villager who had not been in church the previous day, to enquire rather pointedly whether he still liked his cottage.

Henry tried his best to keep the railway, and more particularly their station, out of Sparkford. In view of his objections the railway company carried out a survey with a view to re-siting the station in Queen Camel. When he heard of this, Henry immediately withdrew his objections, rather than see Sparkford's rivals score an apparent victory. Instead, he planted trees on his land bordering the track in the hope that sparks from the locomotives would set them on fire and permit him to claim from the company! Although this did actually occur, it was not until after the Bennetts had sold the estate.

In December 1864 Henry and his wife Emily took up residence in Cannes for the sake of Henry's health. When not confined to his bed, Henry kept busy with his own affairs, but Emily missed English food as she found French cooking too rich for her liking. She obviously hoped they would return to England eventually as she did not buy any clothes whilst she was abroad and feared those she was wearing would not last until her return. It was not to be, however. Henry died on 1st September 1874 aged 79, and Emily on 12th September 1882. They are buried on the north side of Sparkford churchyard, their grave dominated by the tall stone cross on which their names and those of their descendants are inscribed. Nearby, a small grey cross marks the grave of their much travelled nurse, Elizabeth Frances, who wished to be buried close to her former master and mistress whom she had served faithfully for 36 years.

UPHOLDING THE FAMILY TRADITION – HENRY EDWARD BENNETT J.P.

Henry Edward Bennett, Henry's eldest son, was educated at Winchester and progressed to St John's College, Cambridge, where he read law. He was called to the Bar on 16th June 1848. His early life was spent in Canada where he became secretary to Sir James Buchanan Macaulay, Chief Justice to the Court of Common Pleas in Upper Canada. Here, in Toronto, he assisted the Chief Justice to revise the statutes of the Province of Upper Canada. In 1856 he was called to the Bar of Upper Canada and two years later was admitted to practice as a solicitor of the Court of Chancery and attorney of the Court of the Queen's Bench of Upper Canada.

It was whilst he was in Toronto that he met and fell in love with his employer's youngest daughter, Louisa. Henry and Louisa were married in Toronto Cathedral on 26th November 1857. They spent their honeymoon in New York and from there visited England, to arrive on 18th December that year, going straight to Sparkford Hall. It was in 1862 that they finally settled in England after two daughters, Emily and Kate, had been born in Toronto, even though it had been their intention to return to Canada. Their plans had to be changed when Sir James Macaulay died that year and Lady Macaulay arrived in England the year following. In 1863 their first son, Harry Macaulay, was born in Weston-super-Mare, and shortly afterwards they moved to London where, on 4th July 1865, a second son was born, James Buchanan, who died six months later. Sadly, Kate died in April 1866 whilst they were still living in London, and was buried with her brother beneath the chancel in Sparkford Church. Six months later a third son, Frank, was born.

In 1866 the family took up residence at Sparkford Rectory, where four more children were born, Mildred, Edith, Rachael and George. They shared the Rectory with Henry Bennett's youngest son Charles, who at that time was his father's curate and destined to become Rector of Sparkford in 1874. On the death of Henry Bennett, they moved into Sparkford Hall and relinquished the Rectory to Charles.

Henry's legal career now took second place to running the Sparkford Estate. No one in the village questioned his authority and it is said that Henry and Louisa were curiously regal in their ways, being always the 'Squire' and 'The Lady'. Henry is described as being tall and of great dignity, which tended to make him appear somewhat aloof in the eyes of children. He was a great lover of nature and poetry but it is alleged much of his youthfulness and gaiety were masked by shyness, partly by worries due to the agricultural depression, and partly by the responsibilities of a large family and an invalid wife.

Louisa was small and rather delicate, the last years of her life being spent in a wheelchair. She was, however, possessed of an indomitable courage, living up to her family's motto *'Dulce Periculam'* (sweet danger). She died at Sparkford on 12th September 1892 and is buried in the village churchyard. Henry died four and a half years later on 22nd May 1897 at Colwyn Bay, North Wales, and was interred with his wife.

On Henry's death Sparkford Hall was leased, for his sons were settled in the country. Indeed, the burden of debt had become so great that the family were no longer able to maintain the estate. As the Bennetts resided no more at Sparkford the estate was sold at auction during December 1918, against the advice of the family solicitor. With North Cadbury House also disposed of, Somerset no longer provided a permanent home for the family, although a small piece of land in the corner of a field known as Lickhill, was retained as a site for a house at a later date.

THE DISSOLUTION OF SPARKFORD ESTATE
The auction of the Sparkford Hall Estate took place on 17th December 1918. Its total area of 527 acres was broken down into 48 separate lots and sold by Wainwrights & Heard, Surveyors and Land Agents, of Shepton Mallet. Held in Sparkford Schoolroom and commencing at 2pm, the properties under auction comprised Sparkford Hall itself (35 acres), various rich dairy farms such as Brooklands (132 acres), Manor Farm (147 acres), Home Farm (42 acres), Sparkford Grist and Corn Mill, several small holdings and numerous cottages. Their total annual rents, actual, apportioned, and estimated, amounted to £1,461 6s 4d. It is alleged the original title deeds of the local properties had been lost when one of the Bennetts had them in his possession at the time when he was shipwrecked.

Sparkford Hall, together with its 20 acres of timbered park and three closes of rich pasture land that included the plantation cottage was acquired by William D'Oyly Harman, for the sum of £5,000. He had been renting it as a sitting tenant at the time of the sale. It remained in the hands of the Harman family for some while as following William's death, it passed into the hands of his widow, and later to their daughters, the Misses Harman.

One of the Great Western Railway's handsome 'Hall' class locomotives, No. 5997, was given the name *Sparkford Hall* when built in 1940 and would have been seen passing through Sparkford station on occasions when working to or from Weymouth. It was withdrawn and scrapped in 1962 but the two curved brass nameplates are believed to be in private collections today.

The original entrance and driveway to Sparkford Hall no longer exists as the driveway was cut by the new by-pass in 1989. As a result, an entirely new entry to the Hall had to be created. It is now approached off the road to South Barrow, running parallel to the railway and passing under the newly-constructed bypass bridge before it turns to the left off the South Barrow road.

The site of the village pump still exists, where there was also a spring. Although the pump itself (and the spring) have long gone, the inset for the pump in the low wall on the left-hand side of Church Bend (opposite Church Cottage) can still be seen. Electricity came to the village in 1932 but it was some while before it reached the outlying areas.

THE VILLAGE CHURCH – ST MARY MAGDELENE

The Church of St Mary Magdelene is built of stone in the Gothic style. Its date of origin is not known, although records show its first Rector was appointed in 1297. The present building, with the exception of the tower, was mostly rebuilt in 1824 to the design of Thomas Ellis. The perpendicular tower is, however, of 14th or 15th century origin and contains three bells, of which one is pre-Reformation carrying the inscription *Sante Katerina Ora Pro Nobis* (St Catherine, pray for us). The path from the gate to the tower was at one time lined with yew trees and it has been suggested that they were planted there to provide material for the traditional English long bow. In point of fact they were placed there for a more mundane reason. It was difficult to keep cattle out of the churchyard, so they were introduced because yews are poisonous to animals.

The building is of particular interest in having two transept-like structures on the south side (one of which contains the chapel and the organ loft, and the other the vestry). Until 1834 what is now a little chapel, used by some of the Sunday School (and before that as a meeting room), had been the south porch of the church,

A pleasant photograph of Sparkford church taken during the early spring. It shows to advantage the perpendicular tower of 14th or 15th century origin. (Mrs M. Raynor)

Trevor Griffiths (Rector from 1899 to 1940) and his wife Emily outside Sparkford Rectory.

where privileged beggars were allowed to sleep. The chapel's war memorial east window of St Michael and St George is by Sir Charles Nicholson and includes a small panel of glass from Flanders. The east window, which replaced the present west window, is also by Sir Charles Nicholson. It commemorates the Bennett family and depicts the Ascension and was the subject of an objection by the Chancellor of the Diocese on the grounds that there is no biblical authority to substantiate the presence of the Blessed Virgin Mary at that happening.

The organ, formerly at the east end, is now in a loft above the chapel, approached by an outside stone stairway. Purchased in 1911 for £200 it is positioned high in the middle of the south end of the nave, very suitable for congregational singing. At one time there was a band, which played in a gallery under the tower, now removed. The band was later replaced by a barrel organ brought to Sparkford from South Cadbury, its handle turned by Samuel Talbot. On one memorable occasion it refused to stop playing and was carried into the churchyard where it continued to play the 'Old Hundredth' amongst the gravestones!

The pulpit was constructed by James Talbot, the village carpenter, early in the 19th century. It is an assembly of carvings taken from other churches in the area. and used to have coloured panels. The niche Henry Bennett had carved in the north wall on account of his voluminous size when in the pulpit is still in evidence. The interior has, however, changed considerably since the 19th century. Gone is the chancel screen made by James Talbot, and the stove which, in cold weather, stood in the centre of the aisle. Gone also are the long framed panels on which

Helen Bennett (who later became the wife of the Dean of St Paul's) had illuminated the Commandments in her childhood, and the old yellow-painted deal pews. A local farmer regarded their replacements as draughty, and declined attending any further services. When eventually he returned to the fold many years later, he made the mistake of putting a half-crown in the collecting plate under the impression it was only a penny. He put matters right by withholding his contribution for the next 29 consecutive Sundays!

The choir bench ends were taken from old pews in the nave, which were removed at the end of the 19th century. Fixed to an oak slab on the south wall of the chancel is a memorial brass to John Chyke, a Rector who died in 1513. Nearby is the piscina, used for washing sacred vessels. The altar table is probably of the

Emily Griffiths, wife of the Rector, and one of Harry Edward Bennett's daughters. She was well known locally for the tricycle she rode around the village.

An unknown gathering at Sparkford church, with the Rev. Patrick Connor middle right. Also in the group are George Clapp, Herbert Hoskins and Reg Lewis, with Dick Perry and Harry Brain on the extreme right.

17th or 18th century. Other pieces of furniture worthy of note are a prayer desk and a stool and chest close to the door.

Old registers provide few personal portraits of parsons of long ago. One interesting entry relates to Thomas Fry, when instituted by Bishop Buckland in 1445. It reads *On examination he appeared to the Bishop to be hardly sufficiently skilled in letters to have the cure of souls. The Bishop ordered him to attend the schools for two whole years from Michaelmas following, leaving a suitable chaplain in the cure of his church, and to offer himself to the Bishop for examination within a fortnight of the said term.*

Nathaniel Hodges was the Parish Clerk of the 1840s. He lived in the 'back lane' and was heavily involved in cider making. Apart from the Rector he was the most important man in the church, and he made sure no one underestimated his status. When he died in 1852, he was succeeded by Silas Guillford, who tried somewhat unsuccessfully to follow in the same style. Twenty years later, James Talbot became the Parish Clerk, a position he held until his death in 1883, when the post fell into abeyance.

In more recent years Trevor Griffiths O.B.E., M.A., Rector from 1899 to 1940, and his wife Emily (née Bennett) were well known for the tricycles they rode from the Rectory to the church. He was a popular man with local children. If they behaved themselves he would often take them for a ride in his car. He served for a while as the Chairman of Sparkford Parish Council.

Village Buildings and Places of Note

THE POPLARS

Located in The Avenue, immediately opposite the junction with the A359 to Castle Cary and adjacent to the railway, this property is undoubtedly of very early origin as some of the beams used in its construction are believed to have a 15th century origin. In the mid-1850s 'Big' Talbot, nephew of Samuel Talbot, the wheelwright, was the blacksmith. He was also the Parish Constable, though from all accounts not a man of great courage as one might expect. One night he thought he heard some burglars in the house, so he crept downstairs and silently fastened the stair door so that they could do him no harm. Little did he know that they had already fastened the door on the inside, so that he could not get at them! When the stage coaches ceased to run, Talbot sold the smithy and was succeeded by Robert Dampier.

Robert Dampier was clearly a man of determination. He had been courting Joan Sheppard of Marston Magna (the daughter of Thomas Sheppard, the inventor of Sheppard's plough) when her mother took exception and sent her daughter off to Australia. Determined not to lose sight of her, Robert made his own way to Australia soon after and succeeded not only in locating Joan but also in making her his wife in 1858. Four years later they returned to Sparkford with a child and were resident there when Robert died in 1910, the oldest tenant at that time on the Sparkford Estate. The Poplars was bought for £500 by his son, Edwin Dampier, who was the sitting tenant at the time of the village auction. Interestingly, the window frames of the house are made of wrought iron, as befits a house occupied by a blacksmith.

Having served his apprenticeship with Robert Dampier, William Pittard continued the business in the smithy outbuilding at The Poplars. Later, he moved his smithy to the building adjoining Carew Cottage, next to the Sparkford Inn. It was here that he made the gates for Weston Bampfylde Manor.

Around the turn of the century, three separate businesses had been run at The Poplars, those of a blacksmith, wheelright and dressmaker. It is alleged that at one time as many as 25 apprentices had been housed in the roof space. It is also believed what is now the garage may well have been a cider house at one time.

WELL HOUSE

Located next to The Poplars in The Avenue, Well House was at one time the home of Job Hatcher, a pork butcher. It is understood that for a time this property was known as Green Hedges, probably when the main road followed an older and much lower level route before the railway came. It was then much closer to both Well House and The Poplars.

THE SPARKFORD INN

A prominent building on the old London to Exeter road, the Sparkford Inn dates back to the 15th century. Originally the Sparkford Inn and Posting House, it was conveniently located as seven stagecoaches passed daily through Sparkford. Some went to Exeter via Ilchester, whilst others turned off through Podymore and Langport before taking the Exeter road. The 'up' coaches changed horses at the Inn and the 'downs' a little further along the road, towards Wincanton, at the turnpike house now known as The Octagon. The four horses drawing the coach were expected to cover the usual eight-mile stage in order to maintain an average speed of ten miles an hour. This distance was adjusted where steep hills had to be climbed, with relief teams of horses held on 'stand-by'.

From Wincanton to Sparkford the stagecoaches had to descend Blackford Hill. One night during a snowstorm the driver mistook his way. The coach was wrecked at the turning to Blackford Hollow and several of its occupants were killed. A phantom coach was afterwards sighted by travellers on a number of occasions and many local residents were afraid to pass the scene of the accident after dark. The last sighting was reported during the early 1900s, after which road alterations obscured the corner.

The 18th century two-storey livery stables at the inn, with their eight bays, are

A photograph of the Sparkford Inn taken at the time when the Hare's Nest opposite had some of its wares displayed in the garden.

A motorcycle and light car club gathering at the Sparkford Inn. The style of the motorcycles confirms this photograph would have been taken during the mid-twenties.

still evident though they are now converted into garages. The last regular coach to run through Sparkford was routed from Bath to Weymouth, via Frome. It ceased with the coming of the railway.

The future Queen Victoria, then Princess Victoria of Kent, travelled through Sparkford on 23rd December 1819 after she and her parents had spent the night at Ilminster whilst on their way to Sidmouth. She was aged seven months at the time, and it is understood that Henry Stacey, the innkeeper at that time, held her in his arms whilst the horses were being changed.

Soon after the 1914-18 war the inn was acquired by the People's Refreshment House Association Ltd, (as also was the Catash Inn in North Cadbury), the PRHA initials being incorporated in the sign that hung outside the inn. Earlier, the inn was known as the Punchbowle and Posting House and is recorded as such in the 1860s. Robert Dampier, the village blacksmith, held the responsibility for repairs to the stagecoaches, as and when needed. Traces of the 18th century inn can still be found in the staircase (c1800) and in doorways and dadoes.

A little garden opposite the inn (later the site of a wooden building known as the Hare's Nest) was known as the Punchbowle (probably after the former name of the inn itself) and at one time strawberry teas were served there.

An important annual event which started from the inn was the traditional Boxing Day meet of the local hunt, although the inn was the venue for most of their meets in view of its convenient location.

The hunt assembles outside the Sparkford Inn. Date unknown, but the cars and the dress of those present suggests the twenties. Note the unmade road.

This photograph shows the long wooden hut from the Great War that housed various businesses associated with the market.

The hunt returns from across the neighbouring fields whilst the onlookers and supporters bide their time patiently.

John Perry cuts the tape to open the Sparkford Inn's skittle alley. Also in the photograph are Fred Reeves, Dick Perry and Mike Burgess.

A group photograph taken at one of the memorable Hunt Balls held at the Sparkford Inn. The group includes Mike and Runa Burgess, Bob Dyer, John and Ellen Perry, and Dick and Ruth Perry.

The large Agricultural Hall that forms part of the inn was built originally for farmers' meetings. It was also where the annual Hunt Ball was held, organised with meticulous care and enthusiasm by Baruna Burgess (known locally as Runa), Mr and Mrs John Perry's married daughter. It was the Hunt's way of acknowledging the consent of local landowners for them to hunt on their land and Baruna agreed to organise it on the understanding that the ball was to be non profit-making. It was a major event in the village, and many travelled long distances to be there. An awning linked the inn to the hall, and a marquee was erected to join up with the rear of the hall. It was a white tie and tails event, with no exceptions, and it was always a sell out.

The music was provided by top London bands such as Billy Saville, Tommy Kinsman, and the Squadronaires, who started playing at 10pm and continued until 4am. Breakfast was served before everyone left, usually in the form of a very memorable consommée. Many then took part in the hunt that followed, having brought their hunting attire with them.

Other notable annual events held at the inn were the Police Ball, the annual dinner of the local Licenced Victuallers Association, and an annual dinner for the shareholders and staff of the Sparkford Vale Co-operative Dairy Society.

Baser instincts were catered for by the Sparkford Veast. Held opposite the inn,

The joint Huntmasters, John King Brain and Bob Dyer, stand together at the back with Frances King Brain and John Perry next to them. Seated are Mrs Dyer, Ellen Perry, band leader Billy Saville and Runa Burgess.

Some of the happy party-goers at one of the Hunt Balls.

One of the many dinners held at the Sparkford Inn. The group is comprised mostly of farmers and skittlers.

a platform was set up so that cudgel contests could take place. The rules were simple in the extreme – the first one to draw blood was the winner!

SPARKFORD CATTLE MARKET

Sparkford cattle market, of which traces still exist, was located at the rear of the Sparkford Inn. A licence for it was granted in 1632 by the Sessions of the Peace at Taunton to Edward Lidford of Sparkford. It entitled him *to be a maulster and to buy in the open markets at Hindon and Shaston three-quarters of barley weekly to convert into malt, and to sell it again at Sidmouth in Devon, to return thence with his horses laden with salt fish or other commodities, to continue for one year.*

The market as it is best remembered ran from 1922 to the fifties, and on average 600 to 700 calves were sold there each market day. Apart from cattle, the market also catered for sheep, pigs, poultry and rabbits, as well as for produce such as eggs, butter and fruit. Market days were on Mondays, and later on alternate Mondays, which provided time for cattle to be shipped from Ireland and delivered to Sparkford station. They were then driven along the High Street to the market. It was managed from 1919 onwards by Messrs Cooper & Tanner, local estate agents.

Opposite the Sparkford Inn was a public weighbridge, operated by Arthur Neale, who also looked after the cattle market. The key to it was held by the Sparkford Inn.

The 'Triumphal Arch' that formed the original entrance to the long driveway that led to Hazelgrove House.

ENTRANCE AND LODGE TO HAZLEGROVE HOUSE

The main entrance to Hazlegrove House originally comprised an entrance arch (sometimes referred to as the Triumphal Arch), in effect two stone arches (c1690) erected back to back. One account suggests they were brought from Ham Farm in 1872 and had originated from a large mansion which Sir Ralph Stawell was having built for himself in about 1685-90. Another account claims they formed the original gateway to Low Ham Manor, near Somerton, and were acquired by the Mildmay family to enhance the approach to Hazlegrove House. Whichever version is correct, they were used to form the single arch which stands in the village today.

The original driveway to Hazlegrove House was cut when the Sparkford bypass was built in 1989 and in consequence only a very short portion of the original beginning of it now remains. The Lodge, with its distinctive high pitch roof, is a copy of a house in Normandy built by Napoleon III.

The Sparkford bypass necessitated creating an entirely new entrance to Hazlegrove House by making an additional exit off Sparkford roundabout. Interestingly, only the former arch and the lodge are within the Parish of Sparkford as the house itself lies in the Parish of Queen Camel. Hazlegrove House is now a private junior school, part of King's School in Bruton.

CORNER COTTAGE AND THE VILLAGE SCHOOL

On the corner of Church Road (formerly named Sparkford Street), Corner Cottage

An early photograph of Sparkford school and its pupils. The schoolroom occupied the building adjoining Corner Cottage that is now the Parish Hall.

Another view of Corner Cottage with the teachers and pupils lined up outside. The farm waggon making its way up Sparkford Street with a load of sacks is probably heading for the mill. When this photograph was taken, the right-hand corner site was still undeveloped.

A later group of schoolchildren and their teachers outside the school, all in Victorian dress.

Using strips of coloured cloth the pupils of Sparkford school arrange them to make a Union Jack flag. This photograph was taken in 1937.

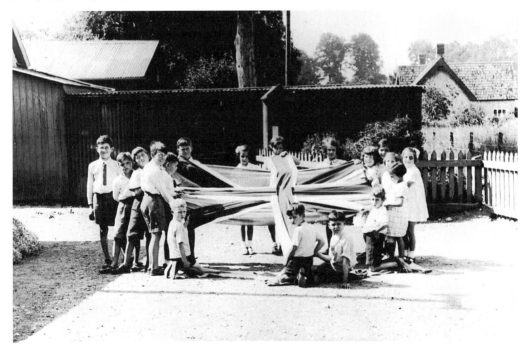

This next group, taken in 1935, will enable those who attended the school that year to identify themselves and their friends!

was at one time the schoolmistress's house, with the school building next to it. The school opened in 1849 and in the 1860s the schoolmistress was Anne Caines of Queen Camel. She was appropriately named too, as she was renowned for not sparing her cane whenever it was necessary to use it.

The school was enlarged in 1892 when it had 80 pupils, accepting children up to the age of eleven. Thereafter, its pupils were transferred to the old school building in Queen Camel. Sparkford school was closed during 1947 when it had only eleven pupils, and thereafter all the village school children, irrespective of age, were transferred to the Countess Gytha School in Queen Camel.

When this change was implemented, the County Council Education Authority decreed the children would have to walk to and from their new school alongside the busy A303, then a major trunk road, because the mileage was below that where they were obliged to provide *free* transport. Their parents took umbrage at this and refused to send them to school in Queen Camel until *free* transport was provided. Their action caused the Education Authority to think again, and after inspecting and measuring the route, they relented six weeks later and agreed they would provide a complimentary bus service after all.

Corner Cottage, at the time of James Hoare's occupancy, was also the site of the village groceries shop. The shop had the agency for supplying provisions to the workhouse at Wincanton.

Also on the same site in the early 1900s was James Hoare's carpenter's shop, to the right-hand side of the house, and to the right of this, the band room used for practising by the Brooklands Band, of which James was its leader. The band room was one of the many former Army sheds that became available after the 1914-18 war. Outside Corner Cottage, close to the junction of Church Road with

The lean-to extension at the front of Corner Cottage at one time accommodated the village shop.

James Hoare carried on his carpenter's business in the building adjacent to Corner Cottage, on the extreme right. A noticeboard between the windows of the two floors proclaims his trade.

After the schoolroom was purchased by the Parish Council in 1952 for future use as the Parish Hall, it was used for all manner of functions. Here is a meeting of the now defunct Sparkford Women's Institute, taken before the main room was rearranged and the old heating stove and its pipe removed.

The Avenue, stood an old field gun which served as a reminder of the war. It was taken away during the World War 2 scrap metal drive.

The school building was sold to Sparkford Parish Council for £200 on 10th July

To help raise money for the Parish Hall's refurbishment, a village Fete was held. Innes Spencer sold the most tickets, to raise a total of £145. He was crowned Garden Prince for his efforts by Dr W. G. H. Hughes, seen here with his wife. Steve Haines (front right) was the runner-up. Also at the presentation were Deborah Walmsley, Helen Saxton and Jennifer Doddington.

A heavy fall of snow and strong winds during the winter of 1977/8 created deep drifts. As can be seen, the Post Office was virtually cut off until the snow could be cleared.

1952 and is now the Parish Hall, the centre for various local meetings and the regular committee meetings of Sparkford Parish Council. Corner Cottage also accommodated for a while the village Post Office after modernisation and the addition of an extension at the rear.

THE OLD MILL

Approached by a track on the right-hand side of the church, the Old Mill is now a private house under which the old mill race still passes, diverted from the River Cam. It is possible this is the mill listed in the Domesday Book, although it is known there was another mill in the vicinity at the same time. In the 1860s John Webber, the miller, was also Churchwarden. He is described as "a man of much dignity, who habitually entered the church just after the Rector had begun the service, then walked slowly up the aisle to his seat, 'smelling his hat' and smoothing it with his elbow before he laid it carefully beside him." Once a year he would attend the Vestry Meeting with his book under his arm, to pass his own accounts and re-elect himself to office before walking back to the mill. No one else ever attended the meeting!

The last miller, Charles B. Anstey, died in 1961. He had two brothers, Bob and Tom. Charlie could not drive, his wife being remembered for the old canvas-topped Bean car she drove regularly. She was renowned for driving on to the Wincanton to Exeter road without ever stopping at the junction! The car was still a runner in 1950 when, after its tyres were pumped up and a new battery fitted, it was driven away by its new owner.

Deliveries of grain were made to the mill by horse and cart from Sparkford railway station but sadly the mill eventually fell into a state of disrepair. It is largely due to the Hutchinson-Brooks who took up occupancy in the 1970s that both the mill and its grounds were restored, even though it was not possible to reclaim the waterwheel that had provided its motive power. Its present occupants are keen to continue with the restoration work.

MANOR FARM

Located in Church Road, Manor Farm was originally the Manor House, destined later to become a farmhouse. Of 17th century origin, the farm was known either as Hill Farm or Sparkford Farm during the 19th century, and the Ordnance Survey map of 1886 clearly refers to it as a combination of both names, Sparkford Hill Farm. The tithe apportionment map and award of 1839 confirms Henry Bennett was the owner of the 175-acre farm at that time, with William Read listed as the tenant farmer. However, as mentioned elsewhere, the title deeds of most of the properties in the village were lost when a member of the Bennett family who was carrying them with him was shipwrecked. As a result it is difficult to trace the history of the farm back beyond 1880 with any real accuracy.

It is known that before the farm was divided in 1835 it comprised a total of 350 acres, at which time it was owned by the Rev. Henry Bennett and James Bennett. They had acquired it from Frances Charlotte Whatmore (formerly a Miss Newman who was by then a widow). She had owned the farm since at least 1766. It is also known that James Bennett had purchased the Lordship of the Manor from the Newman family around 1802. The Newman family are reputed to have owned the Manor at least as far back as 1760. It has also been suggested that the Manor was occupied by members of the Blandford family in the 18th and early 19th century, with the large altar tombs of the family in Sparkford churchyard.

Interestingly, two armorial shields carved in wood are known to have been taken from Sparkford Manor House, being the coats of arms of the Rogers family in Bryanston, Dorset. These suggest the Manor House may be of much earlier origin since one of the shields represents Rogers impaling Hopton. This is of significance as Sir John Rogers married Margaret Hopton in 1609 as his second wife. She died in 1613, so it more closely defines the date of the shield and in consequence may have a direct bearing on the date of the Manor House. It is known that Manor Farm was sold to James Bennett by the Newman family in 1793, and when he died he left it to his son Henry. It was sold much later, in December 1918, for £5,250 with 147 acres of land at the auction of Sparkford Estate.

HOME FARM

Home Farm, next to the old creamery in the High Street, was at one time farmed by the Perry family, who occupied the farmhouse. The farm and its adjoining land realised £4,050 at the village auction in late 1918, and much later the farmhouse was acquired with 4⅓ acres of land on 29th October 1976 by J. H. Haynes & Co. Ltd, after the death of Mrs Ellen Perry. At that time the company desperately needed room for expansion and it was purchased in an after auction deal for £31,000. Although the house itself remained substantially unchanged after planning permission was granted for the change to office use, all of the near-derelict outbuildings were demolished to make room for a 10,000 square foot single-storey printing works, itself later much enlarged. Only the old mounting block and the pump in the yard were carefully preserved.

The adjacent Woodbine and Rose cottages were not purchased at the time of the auction but they too were later acquired by J. H. Haynes and Co. Ltd, and at the time of writing remain unoccupied.

BROOKLANDS FARM

Brooklands Farm is located in Brains Lane, a short unclassified road that originally linked The Avenue with the A359 to Castle Cary (once used by local residents to avoid the congested 'T' junction by the railway bridge at peak holiday times). The road is now a cul-de-sac, with the Sparkford bypass passing above it on a

Farmer Harry Brain was a well-known and very popular person who figured prominently in the life of the village. Very keen on cricket, it was he who gave the field to the Sparkford Cricket Club. The reason for the unusual attire of some of the players is not known, although it may have been for the comic cricket match held on Coronation Day.

Late in life Harry Brain married a Miss Barnes. Here they are both seen on their wedding day being drawn by a ceremonial procession from the yard of Sparkford station to the Sparkford Inn whilst seated in the rear of the car.

Tom Toop, one of the two partners of the London Road Garage, is at the wheel of the car.

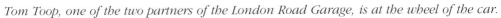

reinforced concrete bridge. Brooklands Farm house was built in 1737 and has two inglenook fireplaces, one of which is still in use. The farmhouse and its 132 acres of land realised £7,900 in the village auction held during late 1918 and was bought by its occupant, John Brain.

During later improvements to the house two bread ovens were discovered, each having a domed brickwork roof. The road has retained the name of the farm's previous occupants, John Brain and then his son Harry Brain. Both were well-known local farmers, the latter having given unstinted service over a long period as Chairman of Sparkford Parish Council. He first held this office in 1934 and continued right through the war years and beyond. Brooklands Farm was often the venue for their meetings.

Harry was also a very keen cricketer and it was he who donated the field which is now the home of the Sparkford Cricket Club. A keen musician, he was the organist at Sparkford Church for a number of years and for a time played in the Brooklands Band which performed at local events. Its leader was James Hoare, and Harry played the violin and his sister the piano. It was late in life that Harry met and married a Miss Barnes, a happy event that the villagers celebrated in a fitting manner.

THE OCTAGON

As will be obvious from its design, this unusual eight-sided house was originally a turnpike or toll house, known to have been in existence in 1643. At this time

A photograph of the Octagon taken before World War 2. It was then a quite separate entity, easily identified as one of the many toll houses that collected revenue from users of the turnpike roads.

the London to Exeter road followed a very different route through the village, having separate 'up' and 'down' roads that passed either side of the turnpike. At one time the house was used as a stopping place where horses on the 'down' stagecoaches were changed. The main road was subsequently made into one in more recent times and realigned, leaving the house more isolated from it in its present position.

In the 1840s the house was occupied by Henry Bannister and his wife. Henry was the village cobbler who made boots by cutting his own leather after measuring a customer's feet with a sliding rule. He used strips of notched brown paper as patterns, which he stored in the roof tresses of the house. Each had the name of the customer recorded on it, so that it was ready for future orders.

For a while, the house was used as the village Post Office, but by the time of the 1918 auction it was known as the Old Post Office and let to James Hancock. It was bought at the auction by John Brain for £350. Later still, it was occupied by a retired naval captain and his lady. Because it had no inside toilet or bath, the Captain screened off a square in the garden, large enough to accommodate a toilet and a shower, with a slatted wooden floor. To take a shower involved releasing a flow of ice cold water from a high mounted water tank on a bracket.

Apparently it was the custom of the Captain to take a shower this way

The Round House was one of the many locations of the village Post Office. It was serving this purpose when the property came up for auction in December 1918. The postal staff show their various forms of transport, one of the postwomen having drawn the short straw with the heavy push cart!

every morning, regardless of the temperature. This was recounted in a letter written during March 1995 to the present occupants by a lady who had stayed there during the early '50s. The vague address she used was itself interesting, being descriptive in nature yet giving sufficient clues to ensure its safe delivery, thanks to the diligence of the local post office. Both the story and the way in which the letter was addressed were featured in the *Daily Mail* and the local press.

Subsequently, the house fell into a state of disrepair. Being a designated Grade 2 building of historic interest it has been restored and incorporated as part of a new dwelling by its present occupants. The remains of various outbuildings can be found in its grounds.

THE ROUND HOUSE

Unfortunately the date of this building is unknown, but it is obviously an old house of the late 18th century, with a thatched roof. Located next to the Sparkford Inn, it has been suggested it may at one time have formed the base of a windmill, but nothing has been found to support this assumption.

At the turn of the century it provided yet another location for the village Post Office, and was still serving the same purpose when it came up for auction in 1918.

Harry Toop had his bakery in Cherry Pie Lane, the narrow roadway off The Avenue, opposite Brains Lane. Originally, deliveries were made by this horse and cart.

Later, Harry acquired this Model T Ford for his deliveries. The bakery also served as another (later) location for the Post Office. Newspapers were often delivered with the bread.

ORCHARD COTTAGE

Orchard Cottage is found in Cherry Pie Lane (sometimes referred to as Bakehouse Lane), a narrow roadway that leads off The Avenue almost opposite Brains Lane. A stone built into the front wall of this cottage leaves no doubt about the date of its erection – 1736. A brick-built extension with a corrugated iron roof was at one time the village bakery, and the property was bought at the 1918 auction for the sum of £190 whilst occupied by Harry Toop. Contemporary photographs show Harry Toop's signwritten Model T Ford delivery van, which delivered with the bread, the *Western Gazette* on its day of publication.

The bakery provided yet another location for the Post Office (and a newsagents), before it moved yet again to Corner Cottage. Eventually the bakery was sold to Harold Lane, who transferred the business at a later date to his cottage fronting the main road in the High Street. The bakery was then removed and replaced by a two-storey extension, with a large window on the ground floor looking out from where the bakery would at one time have stood. Sadly, in late December 1946 Harry Toop was killed when he was knocked off his bicycle by a lorry and trailer on Sparkford railway bridge.

The two adjacent cottages at the entrance to the lane, occupied by Silas Brain and Tom Shean at the time of the auction, were sold to the former for the sum of £350.

HARWARDEN TERRACE

The terraced block of houses known as Harwarden Terrace were sold as a complete unit for £1,000 at the time of the 1918 village auction. They were bought by John Perry, the houses being occupied at that time by sitting tenants who worked for him.

The terrace provided yet another location for the village Post Office, which was combined with a newsagents run by Mrs Ethel Sampson at Number Three.

THE RECTORY

The Rectory, in Ainstey Drive, off Church Road, became the temporary home of Henry Bennett in 1841 whilst Sparkford Hall was being built. It occupied the site of an older building, believed to have been built in 1790. Then a derelict farmhouse fronted by a weed-ridden duck pond, Henry had the pond made into a lawn and the decaying building re-fronted and re-roofed. He also had its approach along a muddy lane transformed into a drive along which trees and laurel shrubs were planted. Henry and his family stayed at the Rectory until Sparkford Hall was completed and they could move in after his mother had died in 1853. Thereafter the Rectory was leased until such time as the properties of the village were sold at auction towards the end of 1918. During the 1914-18 war it had been used as a hospital for the recuperation of servicemen who had been injured whilst on active service.

An old photograph of the Rectory, date unknown. The significance of the banner is unfortunately not known.

A car impressed into the Army to be used as an ambulance during the Great War. Note the portable acetylene light and generator mounted on the offside running board. This car may well have called at the Rectory, which was then used to rehabilitate wounded servicemen.

The Brooklands Band pauses to have their photograph taken in the grounds of the Rectory.
Standing: *Joe Pickford, Ralph Lander, Leslie Giles, Lionel Bailey, Tom Shean, Maurice Neale, Tom Toop and Fred Knibbs.*
Front row: *Fred Andrews, James Hoare (Band Master), Charlie Best and Herbert Biggin.*

A more recent photograph of the Rectory, probably taken before the merger of parishes made it redundant from a clerical viewpoint.

When the parishes were united, the deed for doing so that was drafted some years earlier contained provision that the Rectory of the united parishes should be in Sparkford. Unfortunately, when they were united, the Archdeacon of the day failed in his duty to ensure this was carried out as it is alleged the incumbent at Weston Bampfylde refused to move.

In World War 2 the Rectory was commandeered by the Royal Navy to house a detachment of Wrens. After the war, Owen King had an egg packing station there, using temporary buildings erected in the Rectory's grounds. Eventually the Rectory was sub-divided into flats, occupied by tenants.

THE STEPPES

Found in Church Road, to the right of the junction with Green Close (formerly Gazon Terrace), The Steppes had originally an hexagonal wing to which a further extension has now been added. The house, which at one time had a galvanised iron roof, was approached by a flight of steps off the road, hence its name. It was at one time occupied by Jim Lewis, the village postman.

Gazon Terrace took its name from a close of rich pasture land known as Great Gazons, which sold for £1,600 at the 1918 village auction. Little Gazons adjoined it at that time, itself rich pasture or grazing land that realised £920 at the same auction.

The Steppes, with its corrugated iron roof that replaced the original thatch.

James Ivey poses in his paddock at Oak Cottage, with his donkey and cart. Four small piglets can just be seen in front of one of the cart's wheels.

James Ivey outside Oak Cottage with his two daughters, Frances and Betty.

OAK COTTAGE

Also in Church Road, Oak Cottage has a frontage that is 300 years old, 100 years older than its rear. It featured carved wooden barge boards on the gables. The side windows were added more recently. A former occupant was James Ivey, a carpenter and wheelwright, who kept a donkey in the adjoining paddock. His two sisters, Frances and Betty, ran a laundry from this address and the donkey was harnessed for their collections and deliveries.

HOME COTTAGE

Another property to be found in Church Road, a little further up the road from Manor Farm, was at one time occupied by George and Elizabeth Isaacs and their family, another name associated with business activities in the village. Many years ago, when the cottage's chimney caught fire, the Fire Brigade were called from Castle Cary. To get at the fire they had to break into surrounds that had been added to the fireplace in later years, to expose a vast fireplace and chimney breast. It was so large that when someone looked in to find them, there was not a fireman to be seen. They were all within the vast fireplace and its chimney!

CHURCH VIEW COTTAGES

Their location in relation to Church Road is self-explanatory. They occupy the site of older thatched cottages that were built right up to the roadside. Subsequently destroyed by fire, it is only in more recent years that their replacements have been renovated and modernised.

Mrs Bugler and her cat outside the original Church View Cottages which were later destroyed by fire.

The cottages were adjoined to the north by another cottage that had a lean-to carpenter's shop and shed. At the time of the 1918 village auction the cottage and its land was owned by Charles Gill, and the carpenter's shop rented by James Hoare. The entire lot sold for £350 and was purchased by one of the Ansty brothers.

Although the building is now demolished, Philip Talbot, the village carpenter, had lived there at the turn of the 19th century. His son Samuel, a wheelwright, was accustomed to rising early once a quarter, when he would eat his breakfast, drink a glass of cider, then walk the 25 miles to Bridgwater to purchase what he needed before he walked back home again. The goods would be sent by boat to Langport and a day or two later Samuel would send a horse and waggon to pick them up from the wharf. When the goods arrived in Sparkford he thought nothing of asking his son James to pick up a plough shear and carry it to Bourton where there was an iron foundry. To a young lad carrying a heavy plough shear ten miles, it must have seemed at least five times the distance.

Walking long distances in those days was, of course, quite commonplace. Charlotte Hockey, a glove outworker, thought nothing of walking the nine miles into Yeovil every week to deliver a parcel of finished gloves and bring back a supply of material with which to make more.

Later, Samuel's carpenter's shop was taken over by his son James, a carpenter of outstanding ability. He could build a farm waggon from scratch, including the wheels, and finish it with the traditional painted flourishes. Such was his meticulous attention to detail that he once refused to carry out a little patching work on a worn piece of church flooring, to make it good. His reasoning was, to use his own words, "When I bees in the churchyard the volk will stand by and zay Talbot o'Sparkford did he".

Surprisingly, James' education was interrupted when he had to leave school at the age of eight to look after the baby at home. Growing tired of this unwanted occupation he used to pinch the baby to make it cry, so that his mother would come and take it away. Despite his meagre schooling, he became recognised as a competent accountant and the villagers would take to him their puzzling figures as he was renowned for his fairness and honesty. "We'll bide by what Talbot o'Sparkford do say" said local disputants and even the stewards of large estates would pass his figures and estimates without question if they were aware they had been seen by him.

CAREW COTTAGE

Next to the Sparkford Inn, on the left, is Carew Cottage, originally owned by William Carew, the village blacksmith, and after he had died, by his wife Ann who carried on the business in her own name. It was here that the wrought iron gates

William Pittard, the last of the village blacksmiths, at the gate of Carew Cottage. His smithy adjoining the cottage is seen to the right.

At the far end of the village, close to its boundary with Queen Camel, stands The Mount. Looking both isolated and exposed, its setting is very different today. (Jim Toop)

to Weston Bampfylde Manor were forged by a later blacksmith, William Pittard. The cottage is between 200 and 300 years old. Tom Gray, highly skilled in shoeing horses, will be remembered as one of several of the blacksmith's right-hand men. Much of their work was provided by the local hunt.

Other helpers included Alfie Budgell, who left to work in the creamery and look after its machinery. He remained there until the creamery closed and was unfortunate enough to lose his life many years later in a road accident outside Carew Cottage. Another helper was Len Fennon, who shared a common interest in radio with William Pittard. Together they built several receivers which were used by villagers. Perhaps appropriately, old tractors are now restored in what was once the smithy.

BRIDGE COTTAGE

At one time tea rooms were a familiar sight along most of Britain's main roads, and it was in Bridge Cottage (then known as Bridge House) during the 1930s that Mrs Lily Toop ran the Sparkford Tea Rooms. It was very popular with cycle clubs and recognised by the Cyclists' Touring Club. Located close to the main road bridge over the River Cam, the building had at one time been two separate semi-detached cottages, later combined into one. It has now reverted to private occupation.

Haymaking in the field that adjoins Sparkford Copse. Traditional hayricks, once a familiar sight in the fields, are a rare sight today. (Jim Toop)

Cutting the crops with an old tractor and binder that no doubt had given sterling service for many years. No protective roll bar, let alone a cab, in those days! (Jim Toop)

Reminiscent of a shot of the Somme taken during the Great War, this photograph is of Sparkford Copse after a severe thinning out. John Snow & Co. Ltd, timber and coal merchants of Glastonbury, were its owners at that time. The Copse was once the site of an old quarry and contained a pond with newts that attracted local children.
(Jim Toop)

SPARKFORD RAILWAY STATION

Sparkford railway station, part of the Wilts, Somerset & Weymouth Railway that was later absorbed into the old Great Western Railway network, was opened on 1st September 1856 when Brunel's broad gauge track was laid. It had been intended that the line would terminate at Salisbury, but when the directors became aware that the London & South Western Railway (their greatest rivals) would be extending further west, they decided to continue their own line to Weymouth. The single track, fractionally over seven feet wide, was converted by a massive but well-organised operation to standard gauge in June 1874, during a weekend. The station continued to serve as a passing loop until the track was doubled in 1881, with a cross-over linking the two tracks. It was closed on 3rd October 1966 after the last train had left at 9.30pm, two days earlier. The station buildings and platforms were subsequently demolished as a result of the savage cuts in the

An early photograph of Sparkford railway station. The odd appearance of the track suggests it is laid to Brunel's original broad gauge but this cannot be so. The track was converted to standard gauge in 1874 and the line not doubled until 1881.

A later photograph showing a train approaching the tall home signal taken during June 1915. The width of the openings in the goods shed confirm the track was laid originally to Brunel's broad gauge

Sparkford station staff pose on the 'down' platform, date unknown. They include the roadmen and a shunter with his pole, used for uncoupling goods wagons.

Large quantities of milk were regularly taken to London by train from Sparkford station. In this photograph the milk churns are being off-loaded in the station yard to catch the 3pm train to London, already waiting at the platform.

railway network made by Dr Beeching in an attempt to reduce British Railways' losses. Few traces of the station now remain. Interestingly, the Great Western Railway had used diesel railcars on the line as early as 1935, though not exclusively.

Staffed by a Station Master, a porter/shunter and three signalmen in the '50s, the station had two platforms, the 'up' line having the main station building and a cast iron gentlemen's urinal. Close to its northern end was a goods shed with, at one time, sidings and a single track running into it from points on the main line. The 'down' platform had only a passenger shelter, and close to its northern end, a 24-lever signal box, opened in May 1877. In 1932 a spur off the 'up' line, on the approach to Sparkford station, was laid to the Sparkford Vale Co-Operative Dairy Society's premises, now occupied by the Haynes Publishing Group plc. A small portion of it still remains. John Perry was officially appointed the Great Western Railway's agent for Sparkford.

During World War 2 a siding off the down line on the east side of the station was run into Raymonds timber yard, then being used as an ammunition dump. Much later, during May 1958, a further attempt to reduce losses resulted in a conversion to single-track working from Castle Cary onwards by removing the 'up' line. It is probable this represented the start of a move towards the eventual

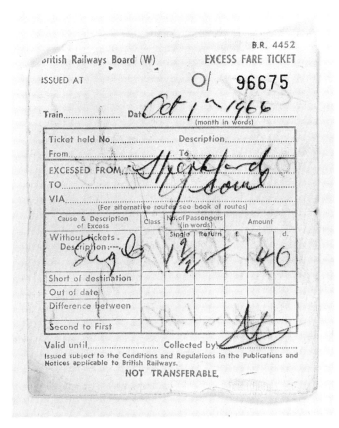

A photograph of the ticket sold for a journey to Yeovil on the last train to leave Sparkford station on 1st October 1966. (Norman Toop)

Taken from the bridge on the A303 that spans the railway, this is one of the last shots to be taken of Sparkford station, which closed on 3rd October 1966. The goods siding had already been removed, goods traffic having ceased on 7th January 1963. Eventually the station itself was demolished and only traces of it now remain. (Colin Caddy)

The bridge over the railway was close to a very tight bend on the A303 and the 'T' junction where it was joined by the A359 from Castle Cary. Many accidents occurred here, of which this is just one. Fortunately the van just missed landing on the track; what fate befell its occupants is not known.

closure of the line as the small number of passing loops along its length to its terminal in Weymouth restricted the amount of traffic it could carry.

Apart from serving as a useful means for the transportation of animals whilst Sparkford cattle market was in use, and for off-loading grain for Sparkford Mill, the station had its own cattle pens and a coal yard. With all its arrivals and departures the station was regarded as a centre for the local community. Even in the very worst of weather, when local roads were either snowbound or flooded, the trains always seemed to keep running.

The road bridge over the railway immediately after the dangerous bend at the junction of the old A303 with the A359 was the scene of many motoring and other accidents, with some vehicles ending up either close to or actually on the railway line itself.

Commercial Buildings, Old and New

SPARKFORD CREAMERY

Land adjacent to the railway line, on the opposite side of the old A303 from Sparkford railway station, was originally occupied by the Somerset Trading Co. Ltd. At one time they traded in a wide variety of products, but by the turn of the century their main business lay in slates and imported timber. The company was owned by Messrs Isaacs & Perry, two local residents. After Thomas Isaacs' death, a 30,000 square foot factory was built on the site by a firm of builders in Long Sutton, to be used for processing milk products. Water for the factory was drawn from the River Cam, where a pumping station had been built close to the bridge

The Sparkford Vale Co-operative Society's creamery is seen on the extreme left with its prominently displayed sign. Next to the factory is Home Farm, the home of John and Ellen Perry. In the foreground is the entrance to Sparkford railway station.

over the road which can still be seen today. The water was carried by a large diameter pipe to the green-coloured tank mounted on the roof of the creamery, after running along the outside of the railway bridge. The water tank, and the whey tank below it, were a familiar sight to users of the old A303.

Founded on 1st April 1918 by John Perry and Ralph Cox, a farming friend of Home Farm, North Cadbury, and registered on the 23rd of that month, the creamery's first year's Annual General Meeting was held on 16th July 1919. It showed the milk processing factory had traded successfully, despite a setback when they found themselves subject to an 80% Corporation Profits Tax. Although contested in court, judgment was given in favour of the Crown. However, by the time of the court case the cause of the problem had already been resolved. Mr E. H. Pope, a cousin of the former Secretary of Aplin & Barrett Ltd, had persuaded John Perry and Ralph Cox to form the Sparkford Vale Co-Operative Dairy Society, of which John Perry became the Secretary and Manager, Ralph Cox a Director and Mr Pope its Chairman. The Rt Hon. Henry Hobhouse P.C. fulfilled the role of the Society's first President.

Under the rules of the new co-operative any person supplying milk had to be a member, which meant taking up at least one share for each milch cow kept. It has been suggested that the Society may well have served as a model for the Milk Marketing Board that came on the scene much later. There had already been a

As smoke drifts lazily across the sky from one of the creamery's chimneys, the hunt makes its way along the unmade High Street. One of the horses seems to be taking exception to the oncoming car. Note the prominent water and whey tanks, recognised 'landmarks' by all who travelled west on the A303.

Charlie Penny, the Chief Engineer at the creamery, is presented with a long service watch. John Perry, the company's secretary and manager, is standing on the right.

move towards a suggested amalgamation of the National Farmers Union and the United Daries to consolidate this country's milk industry, but the newly-founded Society was not in favour.

In 1922 the Society suffered a setback resulting from a fire in the engine house caused by a spark from a diesel engine driving the cooling and other plant. Fuel oil stored in barrels near by ignited and the fire quickly spread from the roof of the engine house to the delivery section of the creamery. The Yeovil Fire Brigade arrived within a half hour and had the fire under control within an hour, managing to save the adjoining cheese factory as well as John Perry's stables. The engine house was, however, completely destroyed and the building gutted. All the machinery inside was damaged and the stock ruined. Fortunately, the day's milk had already been despatched, although the fire had its effect on the London milk trade, where the Society had a depot.

Many years later, when the Milk Marketing Board had cut the profit on milk to two pence a gallon, the Co-operative found itself running at a loss and by 1936 had an overdraft of over £15,000. At a special meeting held on 22nd March 1937 to discuss the sale of the Society, the then President, Sir Archibald Langman, Bt, CMG, put it to the meeting that the only sensible option would be to sell out and accept an offer made by Messrs Aplin & Barrett. Asked by a shareholder why the Society had gone into decline such that it had now become necessary to wind it

Charlie proudly displays his watch with a group of factory employees. Brenda Best is next to him. No need to identify the occupation of the person on Charlie's right. The oil-stained overalls leave no doubt that like his colleague on Brenda's left, Alfie Budgell, is also a maintenance engineer!

up, Sir Archibald gave what he believed to be at least two valid reasons. Firstly, they had no proprietary articles to sell as compared to other dairies, and secondly their overheads had been high because they did not deal with enough milk. Only the big companies such as Aplin & Barrett and Kraft were able to make money out of manufacturing.

Aplin & Barrett had been the only company to offer to purchase the Society's assets in their entirety, for the sum of £39,230, which included their depot in London. This offer was made on the assumption that the creamery would continue to operate much as before and that its senior management would remain to provide continuity during the change-over period. The meeting was in favour of accepting Sir Archibald Langman's proposition, which included part of the purchase sum being paid in the form of £7,846 worth of Aplin & Barrett Preference Shares which he had negotiated for the benefit of the Society's shareholders. The final shareholders' meeting was held on 17th June 1938, at which the liquidator's report was presented and accepted.

John Perry continued as Manager of the factory until his retirement in November 1958. Now under the once familiar St Ivel name, it eventually became part of the Unigate Group, and when rationalisation of the latter's production facilities took place during the late '60s, the creamery was closed and put up for sale.

A keen horseman who rode regularly with the hunt, John Perry is seen here in his stable yard with Smokey. Nettles is in the stable behind him, a horse ridden with considerable success by his son Dick.

A very young Jack Sugg with his father. The rear end of John Perry's old solid tyred Vulcan lorry can just be seen in the background.

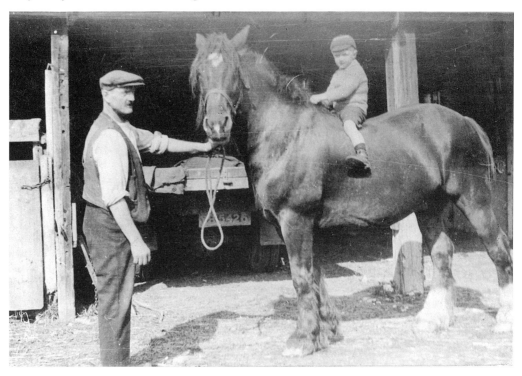

John Perry, the driving force behind the Sparkford Vale Co-operative Dairy Society, died aged 87, his loss keenly felt by the village in which he had played a leading role since his first tentative venture into business by selling apples. He left a wife and a daughter as sadly he had been pre-deceased by his only son Dick, who had died in the mid-sixties.

Like his father, Dick was no mean horseman and from an early age had enjoyed many successes in local riding events. Later, he progressed sufficiently well to ride with the professionals and was soon in demand to compete in horse events all over the country. He also followed in his father's footsteps and served on Sparkford Parish Council.

Dick died whilst still in his forties, leaving his wife Ruth and two sons, Nigel and Richard Jnr. and a daughter Helen. They lived in Rose Cottage, adjacent to Home Farm in which his parents resided.

In 1971 fortuitously, J. H. Haynes & Co. Ltd, a local printer and publisher of car and motorcycle workshop manuals and books, were at that time desperately in need of room for expansion, and on the return of John Haynes and his family from their first trip to the USA it was with delight and excitement to see a large 'For Sale' sign outside the creamery. Although not ideally suited to their requirements, the advantageous price for the purchase of the freehold could not be ignored compared with what would be required for a new unit on an industrial estate. It

The green-painted water tank remained a familiar sight to users of the old A303 until it was removed after the creamery was acquired by the Haynes Publishing Group.

The new reception area of the Haynes Publishing Group which stands on the site of Home Farm's old milking parlours. The oblong-shaped two storey building in the right background is the only part of the old creamery that has an unchanged exterior.

is therefore perhaps a little ironic that at the winding up meeting of the Society, Sir Archibald Langman had said he could not envisage any other purpose for which the factory building would be suited! The premises were bought by Haynes and after a number of internal modifications and the removal of the tanks on the roof, the company transferred its operations from West Camel and Lower Odcombe, to take up occupation early in 1972.

The acquisition of the old Unigate premises proved the turning point in the company's fortunes, leading to the formation of the Haynes Publishing Group plc in 1979, a publicly-owned company with its shares quoted on the London Stock Exchange. The story is told in a 120-page fully illustrated book entitled *Haynes: The First 25 Years,* published in 1985 to commemorate the Group's 25th Anniversary.

The company specialises in the origination and publication of car and motorcycle owners workshop manuals, having its own printing facilities, as well as a comprehensive range of hardback books relating mostly to motoring and motorcycling topics, railways, and leisuretime pursuits. It is also very active in America through Haynes Publications Inc., with premises on the outskirts of Los Angeles and in Nashville, Tennessee.

Richard Noble, holder of the World Land Speed Record at 633.468 mph, about to cut the tape to open the Sparkford Motor Museum as it was then called. The World Land Speed Record achieved by Richard in October 1983 whilst driving Thrust 2 *still stands today.*

THE HAYNES MOTOR MUSEUM

Located off the A359 to Castle Cary, on a site originally occupied by a succession of timber yards and sawmills, the Haynes Motor Museum came into existence in 1985, comprising a large collection of cars owned by John Haynes, O.B.E., Chairman of the Haynes Publishing Group.

It was officially opened on 10th July 1985 by Richard Noble, holder of the World Land Speed Record, by which time it had assumed Registered Charitable Trust status. A further, later, acquisition of land from Sparkford Sawmills Ltd permitted a significant extension of the original building. The extensively re-modelled Museum, now a major tourist attraction, was officially opened on 11th July 1995 by Murray Walker, O.B.E., BBC Television's motor sport commentator. The occasion coincided with the Haynes Publishing Group's 35th Anniversary, the 10th Anniversary of the original opening of the Museum, and John Haynes' recent award as an Officer of the Order of the British Empire in the Queen's Birthday Honours List.

The Museum is in regular use as a starting or finishing point for car and motorcycle related events, for hosting visits by one-make clubs, for autojumbles, and for virtually anything connected with mechanised transport. It has its own video cinema, cafe and a retail bookshop.

John and Annette Haynes leave the Longleat stage in the Museum's white Jaguar XK150. The event is one of the annual Haynes Classic Car Tours.

Murray Walker, O.B.E., the famous television Formula 1 Grand Prix commentator, about to open the Haynes Motor Museum's new Reception Area, Dawn of Motoring display, and the New Hall, on 11th July 1995.

Adjacent to the museum is a test track with one kilometre of tarmac, on which exhibits from the museum can be demonstrated. In consequence it is a 'working museum' with virtually all of its exhibits fully restored to a very high standard and maintained in full running order.

SPARKFORD SAWMILLS LTD

There have been sawmills on the site adjoining the railway line, only a short distance up the A359 in the direction of Castle Cary, for something like 60 years. After many changes in ownership, and a period during World War 2 when the site became an ammunition dump, the sawmills have been owned by the Minto family since 1971. Before that, they had a sawmill at Ubley, but when they needed to expand they decided to move to the Sparkford site on the understanding that they would also be able to build six houses there. The move cost them £25,000, and it was to their dismay that once they had settled in, the Department of the Environment revoked any possibility of the houses being erected.

Initially there were two separate sawmills, Charles Franks Limited owned by Norman Minto, and Sparkford Sawmills Limited owned by his son Bryan. They were complimentary to each other as Charles Franks Limited acted as wholesalers, and Sparkford Sawmills Limited as a retailer. Of the two businesses, only Sparkford Sawmills Limited now remains. The Charles Franks site was acquired to house the original Sparkford Motor Museum collection, and later, part of the Sparkford Sawmills site was also acquired, so that the museum could be further extended.

The company manufactures on site a wide range of high quality products, comprising individually designed staircases, windows in a variety of styles, fencing, traditional doors, gates of all kinds and wooden buildings.

WOODSIDE FARM

Woodside Farm, on the left-hand side of the A359 road to Castle Cary, was started in 1880 and initially went through hard times. Perhaps appropriately, it was then known as Starve-a-Lark Farm. Two years later the Saunders family moved in from Leigh, near Sherborne. Hannah Saunders was first listed as the farmer and later, Henry T. B. Saunders.

In 1928 Mrs Kate Saunders acquired a coal yard about 50 yards from Sparkford railway bridge, fronted by a stone wall, on the left-hand side of the A359. It was on the other side of the railway, opposite the coal yard owned by Isaacs & Perry. Miss Ruth Saunders was the first woman in the area to drive a coal lorry and to ride a motorcycle. K. Saunders later acted as general hauliers, this extension to the business being directed from the farm further up the road to Castle Cary.

LANE'S BAKERY

Lane's Bakery, run by Harold Lane, was located in the High Street, almost opposite Carew Cottage. It was closed in 1960, and the baking ovens removed soon after. The cottage to which the bakery was attached was later demolished as it had been

Ruth Saunders was not the only woman to ride a motorcycle locally, although she may well have been the first. May and Ena Toop are seen here with their motorcycles in the lane leading to the bakery. The machine on the right is quite rare, a Wooler, made in small numbers at Alperton, Middlesex. Finished in yellow and black, it was known as 'the flying banana'!

There was also a coal yard on the other side of the railway, opposite that of K. Saunders. In later years it was owned by John Snow & Co. Ltd, of Glastonbury. David Baker and the late Roy Catton are with one of the delivery lorries in this post-World War 2 photograph.

Harold Lane and his family. They ran the bakery situated almost opposite Carew Cottage in the High Street.

built right up to the road's edge and delayed the road being widened. New houses that lay further back were built on its site.

THE HARE'S NEST
At one time, two buildings of wooden construction fronted the main road, opposite the Sparkford Inn. On the left of what is now the main entrance to the Haynes Publishing Group was an antiques shop known as the Hare's Nest, which displayed its name on a free-standing pub-like sign. It was owned by Captain and Mrs Alexander. The site is now part of Haynes Publishing Group's car park, by the bus stop. Traces of the former property still remain in the form of the stone boundary wall and its gateway entrance by the bus stop.

THREE BANKS, A SOLICITORS, A GRAIN STORE AND A DAIRY SHOP
Another wooden building, originally an army hut transferred from Salisbury Plain after the 1914-18 war, was located to the right of the present entrance to the Haynes Publishing Group's site. It was put there to be in close proximity to Sparkford cattle market and at first it was occupied by what was known as the Farmers Depot. Later it was subdivided and extra doors added, to provide access to branches of the Westminster Bank (c1927), Lloyds Bank (c1931) and Barclays Bank (c1931). Another section was occupied firstly by Dyne, Hughes, Archer and Francis, Solicitors and Commissioners for Oaths, and then by Woodforde and Drewett, of the same profession. There was also a grain store run by Isaacs & Perry

The original ex-Great War long wooden army hut that once occupied the area which is to the right of the present entrance to Haynes Publishing. At first used as a grain store, the hut was later sub-divided into separate units and occupied by three banks and a firm of solicitors.

Later, a dairy shop was opened on the same site, moved from the grounds of Home Farm. Another of John Perry's enterprises, he is seen here with Harry Brain on the right.

Edgar Knight of Queen Camel used this delivery van to supply groceries locally. His shop in Queen Camel High Street still exists today, though now under different ownership. Before it was sold, its interior was like a time warp from the days of the Ebdon brothers, its original owners. It is a pity it was not preserved as a complete unit.

at the rear. When eventually the occupants moved out, part of the hut became a barber's shop.

A later addition was a dairy shop, transferred from a temporary building in the grounds of Home Farm. Smart in its white and green livery, it was subsequently replaced by a more permanent building that stood in front of the original long hut that contained the banks and the solicitors. It remained there until the site was cleared and new houses took its place.

SPARKFORD'S GARAGES

The arrival of the motor car and the increasing amount of traffic on one of the main holiday routes to the West Country eventually led to the establishment of two garages in the village. The first, London Garage, was built in 1927 at a cost of £300. It adjoined the ex-WD wooden shed from the 1914-18 war period which had become the home of the Windsor family, part of the shed having been developed into a village shop that contained the Post Office for a while and also a Labour Exchange. The garage, which fronted on to The Avenue, was owned by Tom Toop and Tom Windsor and had the usual forecourt and repair facilities, approved by both the AA and the RAC. Part of the premises were taken over during World War 2 by the Fleet Air Arm for the rebuilding of aircraft engines.

Tom and Cyril Toop with one of the mechanics, astride an old motorcycle on the forecourt of London Garage. Note the old petrol pumps and the bins containing oil dispensers.

A young Jim Windsor outside the wooden hut that was the family home. It was yet another of the ex-Army buildings sold after the 1914-18 war.

Tom Windsor, who went into partnership with Tom Toop to give Sparkford its first filling station.

The ex-Army wooden hut served a multitude of purposes. Apart from being the home of the Windsor family, part of it also served as the village store and Post Office. At one time it even housed the local Labour Exchange!

The name of one of the original partners lives on in the hands of Jeremy Windsor, who specialises in lawnmower sales and repairs. He occupies the site immediately opposite the old Windsor & Toop garage, where at one time could be found the garage's second set of petrol pumps on the northern side of the A303.

A second garage appeared a few years later, owned by Claude and Wilfred Burgess, who had been listed as motor engineers since the early 1920s. This garage offered similar facilities and was AA approved. It was sited at the western-most end of the village, in the apex where the A359 originally joined the A303. The site was originally known as Sparkford Cross, marked by a small grassy mound.

A wooden building alongside the garage, another relic of 1914-18 war, was occupied by Charles Hancock, who specialised in electrical work and took in work from neighbouring counties. Originally from Wiveliscombe, he lived in Lime Kiln, a house with its drive fronting on to the A359, opposite the junction with Sparkford Hill Lane, the minor road that leads to Sparkford Copse.

The garage was subsequently acquired by Reg Wake in 1959, to fend off a rival bid from John Knight of Yetminster. Both were already running coach services and Reg Wake had been garaging his own fleet in the wooden building adjoining the garage which he had bought from Charles Hancock in 1940.

Reg Wake had started his company in 1930, operating from premises in South Barrow. His first coach was a Ford Model T charabanc he bought from Tom

The heavy snowfall of the winter of 1977/8 blocked the A303 and the A359, mainly because high winds had caused deep snowdrifts in places. An attempt is being made by a JCB to clear the A359 at its junction with the A303. Wisely, Wake's Garage stays closed for the time being.

All roads lead to Rome. The just re-opened A303 could have proved misleading to early users whilst snow still covers the first letter of the direction sign to Frome!

Windsor. The service covered North and South Barrow and was of great value in linking all the local villages on market day by extending the run to Shepton Mallet and Yeovil.

The acquisition of the complete garage proved an ideal relocation as the village bus became an even more vital service to the local community after the railway station at Sparkford was closed during late 1966. It is alleged Southern National were none too pleased by this intrusion into what they had come to regard as their territory so they re-planned their timetable to ensure their buses departed five minutes before Wake's. The villagers were wise to this, however, and would stand back to let the rival bus depart so that they could catch the Wake's coach they preferred to patronise.

The Sparkford Bypass – A 75-Year Saga

It is understood the need for a Sparkford bypass was discussed during the early twenties. With the main London to Exeter road (A303) passing through the centre of the village and the ever-growing volume of traffic, especially when holiday traffic was at its peak, it became even more of a necessity a decade or so later. Surprisingly, a proposed route was plotted to the left of the village when heading west, even though it would cut the village in half. Accordingly, a gap was left for it in 1938, when new houses were being built in Church Road (then Sparkford Street). Whatever plans may have been laid they had to be abandoned due to the outbreak of war a year later. Unfortunately, the subsequent and later

Sparkford Street (renamed Church Road) as it used to be, long before the need arose for a bypass. As can be seen in this photograph, the road is still unmade.

filling in of the gap between two of the houses led to a numbering system that even today causes confusion to anyone making deliveries who is not familiar with the arrangement.

After a long period of enforced austerity it was not until late 1953 that the bypass again came under discussion, by which time it had been agreed the A303 would assume trunk road status in preference to the A30. The Ministry of Housing and Local Government gave notice of their intention to hold a public local enquiry into the Somerset County Development Plan at the Shire Hall, Taunton, on Tuesday, 9th February 1954. Since this would include discussion on the proposed route of the new trunk road through Sparkford, a special meeting was called by the Parish Council to be held in the Parish Hall on 30th January 1954. As anticipated, objections were strongly voiced by local farmers and businessmen whose livelihood would be threatened by this development. As a result, it was arranged for those affected within the area covered by the town map of Yeovil to make their representations at the Council Chamber of Yeovil's Municipal Offices on 1st March rather than at the Shire Hall in Taunton.

The route to be taken by the bypass was of vital interest to local farmers, who stood to lose some of their best land and end up with fields of unusual shape that were economically unworkable. John Perry, of Home Farm, and Harry Brain, Chairman of Sparkford Parish Council, were just two of many so affected. The Somerset South East Group of the National Farmers Union filed their own objection and supported the farmers by appointing Messrs Clutton & Hippisley of Wells, Surveyors, Land Agents and Auctioneers, to comment on three separate schemes that had been proposed for the bypass. Meanwhile, Lt. Cmdr. Lynch Langdon, the local member of Parliament, had already been approached by John Perry, Commander Cross of Orchard Cottage, and others, to canvas his support.

All three schemes involved building an extra railway bridge alongside the existing one to create a one-way system and a roundabout at the eastern end of the railway crossing. Scheme One would certainly not have been very popular as it would have cut right across the cricket ground! Inevitably, the Minister was slow to make a decision and hinted it was unlikely it would be made until at least the middle of 1955.

All then went quiet for a lengthy period, presumably because local residents still insisted improving the existing A303 would prevent the unnecessary upheaval of village life. It was not until 1977 that the subject again came to the fore when the Department of Transport (who had by this time taken over the responsibility for road strategy) published details of three alternative routes for the proposed bypass.

The amount of traffic passing through the village was by now causing concern, much of the increase due to closure of part of the county's railway network. A public meeting was held in Sparkford Parish Hall on 10th February to discuss the Department's A303 Trunk Road Improvement Scheme, all three routes of which would divide the village by passing to its south. The meeting was followed by an exhibition in the Parish Hall on 16th and 17th February, when the three routes could be viewed and discussed in detail.

The Blue Route ran to the left of, and adjacent to, Sparkford Hill Lane for most of its route, before it cut across the A359 by Hill View council houses in Queen Camel to rejoin the existing A303 at Conygore Corner. The Yellow Route followed the Blue Route from Chapel Cross, then passed close to the Southern Electricity Board's sub-station at the end of Church Road, before it cut through Wolfester Terrace to join the A303 by the old Frying Pan Cafe. The Green Route ran close to the existing A303, missing the centre of the village by cutting through Church Road, more or less following the pre-war route.

Local opinion remained strongly in favour of improving the existing A303 and recommended the Department's whole project ought to be re-thought. It was even suggested the plans should be put on hold until it was known how traffic flow in the area would be affected by the soon to be opened M5 Motorway. If a bypass were to be constructed, a northern route would have a far less damaging effect on the community.

Formed a short while afterwards, the Sparkford Action Group distributed a questionnaire to local residents. The results confirmed they were in favour by a ratio of 4.2:1 of a northern route. Advised about this, the Director of the South Western Road Construction Unit of the Somerset County Council agreed to fully evaluate this alternative proposal before a decision was made on the preferred route. It led to a further public meeting in Sparkford Parish Hall on 6th July 1977, with representatives from the Department of Transport. Their objections to a northern route were made mostly on grounds of cost effectiveness, even though local opinion remained resolutely in favour of it.

A second public consultation took place at the Sparkford Inn on 28th/29th November 1978, accompanied by another exhibition. Revised plans revealed the Yellow Route was unchanged from that shown in the earlier proposal as was also the Green Route. Now, for the first time, and to everyone's surprise, a Pink Route had been added to the north. It would involve building an extra railway bridge close to Sparkford Sawmills, and new entrance roads to Hazlegrove House and Sparkford Hall. Although it received the majority vote it at first seemed unlikely it would be adopted due to economic constraints, but when the Somerset County Council announced their decision during August 1980, it came as a pleasant surprise that they were at last in favour of a route to the north.

After protracted discussions and negotiations the Department of Transport finally issued plans for the Pink Route in January 1988. Construction commenced during September that year, after a ceremony at which Robert Boscawen, the local Member of Parliament, was present. The new dual carriageway bypass was officially opened on 25th October 1989 by Robert Atkin, the then Minister of Transport.

The design and supervision of the £7.5 million scheme was entrusted to MRM Partnership, the Department of Transport's engineers. They in turn contracted the work to DMD Limited. To the latter's credit the new three-mile bypass was completed some eight months ahead of schedule.

A projected further extension of the dual carriageway from the roundabout at the end of the Sparkford bypass to the commencement of the Ilchester bypass will necessitate further realignment of the A303 in the vicinity of the Sparkford roundabout. In effect, this will isolate the existing roundabout as the realigned road will pass to the north of it, taking more land from the approach to Hazlegrove House.

Although there will be a slip road from the A359 to take westbound traffic on to the A303 without having to pass through Sparkford, there is no provision for a similar slip road for eastbound traffic. If a change in plans is not made to address this problem, heavy traffic heading in that direction will again have to pass through the village to gain access to the A303, via the spur off the A359 in the vicinity of Sparkford Sawmills. Sadly, at the time of writing the Highways Agency seem to regard such an obvious necessity as having a low priority, despite intense local representations.

Meanwhile, proposals for a 30mph limit through the village have been rejected despite strong local lobbying, so that the only viable alternative would appear to be a traffic calming scheme along the High Street. Interestingly, a proposal for a 30mph speed limit was made as long ago as March 1952 by Mrs Agnes Pittard, and it met with similar opposition by those responsible for implementing any such change at that time.

The Sparkford Vale Harriers

The shire counties have always shown a keen interest in field sports, especially hunting, and in this respect Sparkford was no exception. When permission to hunt in Sparkford Vale, an area of some 20 square miles, had been given by Mr Merthyr Guest in 1888, the Sparkford Vale Harriers was started by Mr H. Turner of Cary Fitzpaine. The pack were for a time kennelled at Wales, Queen Camel, where a skeleton pack was maintained throughout World War 2, even though it was no longer possible to hunt. The Master of the Hounds was Major Hodgson, of Eyewell House. After the war, more hounds were added to the pack and by the 1948/9

The hunt passing along the High Street was once a very familiar sight.

This photograph, taken close to the Sparkford Inn, shows the end of the long wooden hut in the High Street that contained Barclays Bank, and also John Perry's Dairy Shop in its final resting place. Note also the old Sparkford Inn sign on the left.

season it comprised 40 Stud Book Harriers, with hunting days on Wednesdays and Saturdays. Amongst their many activities, the Harriers also held an annual Point-to-Point meeting at Babcary and, of course, their memorable Hunt Balls in the Agricultural Hall of the Sparkford Inn.

The Sparkford Vale Harriers ceased to exist as a separate entity when, in 1971, they were combined with the Blackmore Vale Foxhounds.

Sparkford in World War 2

Quite apart from the ammunition dumps spread around the immediate area, the close proximity of Yeovilton aerodrome and its satellite at Sigwells, and the many members of the armed forces in local camps, Sparkford also became the wartime home of many children evacuated from London.

The September 1989 issue of *Landworker* provides a typical account of life at that time seen through the eyes of Ted Marsh, a Londoner who was evacuated to Sparkford on 1st September 1939 as one of 300 children. He lodged with Reg Hobbs and his wife and spent 5½ years in the village, during which time he developed a real love of the countryside. Although he returned to his native city in May 1945, he found himself so restless that he could no longer settle there. He returned to Sparkford where he married the daughter of a farmworker, the Secretary of the North Barrow branch of the NUAAW, and in 1952 became Secretary himself.

Sparkford had its own Home Guard detachment, which was active from 15th June 1940 to 31st December 1944. It comprised the following:
> *Back row:* G. Fowler, J. Dyke, C. Mitchell, R. Hobbs, J. Bird, D. Cluett, H. Hoskins, R. Payne, T. Edwards, J. Coleman, A. Alexander, ? and R. Chivers.
> *Middle row:* D. Stevens, J. Morrison, B. White, B. Hebditch, R. (Dick) Perry, B. Osborne, H. Lane, F. Reeves, B. Bishop, D. Green and T. Perry.
> *Front row:* H. House, M. Toop, J. Sugg, R. Brooks, F. Pomeroy, A. Budgell, C. Penny and H. Lintern.

Local Stories and Personalities

Almost opposite the gates of Hazlegrove House at one time stood some cob cottages, which were pulled down in 1880. Constructed of mud and a foundation of brick or stone it was in one of these that Bampfylde Moore Carew lived, the so-called King of the Gipsies. Born in Devon during 1699 of a well-to-do family he was educated at Blundell's school in Tiverton, from which he ran away to join a band of gipsies as the result of some unrecorded incident. Subsequently he travelled to Newfoundland and after his return to England he married the daughter of a Newcastle apothecary, passing himself off as a mate in the merchant navy.

A series of frauds resulted in him being transported to Maryland where, after escaping from a penal settlement, he secured a passage home by posing as a Quaker in Pennsylvania. Back in England he had a narrow escape from a press gang, which he averted by pricking his face and rubbing in a mixture of salt and gunpowder to give the appearance of smallpox. Thereafter he roamed Somerset, maintaining himself by trickery. His frauds were so ingenious that his victims invariably treated him with great tolerance.

When Claude Patch died, the west country gipsies elected Bampfylde Carew as their 'King' and it was his boast that he could practise every gipsy art as skilfully as any Romany. He is said to have reformed his ways in later life after winning a large sum of money in a lottery, and died in about 1758. There were Carews in Sparkford from at least 1789 to 1918, but the similarity may have been no more than a coincidence as Carew is a well-known West Country surname.

With regard to more recent times, Jim Windsor recounts something that happened when he was a young lad. It relates to Emanuel Shackell, one of two brothers who worked for Mr Saunders, a local farmer. Early one morning Jim saw him staggering down the centre of Sparkford Street dragging a heavy metal trunk which was secured around his waist by a strong rope. He waited until Jim's grandfather had opened the Post Office and was able to help him carry the trunk inside. On opening it, both Jim and his grandfather were dumbfounded to find it filled with coins, many of them gold sovereigns!

It seemed that Emanuel, the owner of this treasure trove, wished to pay his savings into the Post Office Savings Bank for safe keeping as previously the trunk had been buried in the garden. Wisely, Harry Toop decided it was too large a sum to invest in this manner, so the trunk and its contents were taken by car to Castle Cary and used to open an account in one of the banks.

Loyalty was always strong amongst local farmworkers, and clearly Herbert Lintern was no exception. Employed as a carter at Little Weston Farm, he was awarded a Long Service Medal by the Royal Agricultural Society in 1952 for working on the farm for 58 consecutive years. Born in Blackford, he continued working on the farm in his later years, on a part-time basis, to record a total of 65 years service in total before he finally retired completely.

Another local farmworker who may well have qualified for a long service award was Sam Chamberlain, had he not been made redundant in 1964. Having worked out of doors in all weathers, it seemed an almost natural change of occupation to become a postman. Little could he have realised at the time that he would be delivering the mail for a further 24 years, the last two of them in Sparkford.

Sam Chamberlain comes back from his morning round delivering Sparkford's post. The A303 was always busy and inclined to prove hazardous to cyclists.

Jeremy Windsor makes a 21-years' service presentation to Mrs Prowse at Sparkford Post Office. Although she lived in Queen Camel, Mrs Prowse delivered Sparkford's post for a while.

Enforced retirement eventually brought his working days to an end, after the postal services were reorganised and henceforth all deliveries were to be made by van.

A dedicated cyclist, Sam averaged a distance of 40 miles a day on his bicycle and was never defeated, even by bad weather. If there was a heavy snowfall he cut across the fields to make sure our mail reached its destination on time. He admits to at one time having tried a motorcycle, but as it made him cold he quickly gave it up. As for cars and the like, he never showed any interest in them at all. His 21 years service with the Post Office was marked by the presentation of a certificate at Sparkford Post Office. Mrs Prowse of Queen Camel, who also delivered the post in Sparkford for a while, was another who received a certificate to commemorate her 21 years of service.

Also to be remembered is one of many earlier postmen, Jim Lewis, who lived in The Steppes. His round took in Sutton Montis such that he had to walk a considerable distance, bearing in mind two daily deliveries were made in those days. His son Reg had been gassed in the 1914-18 war but it did not prevent him from following in his father's footsteps. He later became Clerk to Sparkford Parish Council.

Although Sparkford never had its own resident policeman, it did have its Special Constables, Tom Toop and Tom Windsor. Also in this group can be seen Len Baber, John King Brain, Wilf Spencer and Eric Hill from the neighbouring villages.

Coach outings were frequent, in what was then known as a charabanc. This men's outing to a now unknown destination has many well-known local residents as passengers. Charabancs from Bird Brothers of Yeovil feature in many old photographs.

Long service on the railway was by no means uncommon either. During December 1919 Mr E. P. Smart, a resident of Sparkford, died only a few days short of his 102nd birthday. He had joined the railway in 1839, a year after its opening and in 1892 had retired at the age of 74 whilst in the position of Permanent Way Ganger of the Great Western Railway's Engineering Department. Like so many families employed by the railway, his sons had followed in his footsteps. His grandson was a linesman's assistant in the Signal Department at Tiverton Junction and his great grandson was a clerk in the goods department at St Davids station, Exeter.

Although Sparkford had its own Special Constables, it did not have its own resident policeman. In consequence many will recall P.C. Dennett, who was based in Marston Magna. In those days the law was treated with the greatest of respect and feared by all who erred in their ways. Jim Windsor can recall being warned on at least two occasions about riding his bicycle without lights after lighting up time. On the third occasion, P.C. Dennett dispensed summary justice by dealing him a hefty clout around the head with his cape. The cape's chain caught Jim's ear and he recalls how it made it 'sing' for some while afterwards! P.C. Dennett gave the area 23 years dedicated service before he retired in 1960.

One wonders what would have happened to P.C. Dennett had he have treated one of today's delinquents in a similar manner – and what the receiver of such rough justice would have been paid in compensation!

Anecdotes about the villages in the Sparkford area, including Sparkford itself,

This earlier photograph shows an even older charabanc with solid rubber tyres. It would have given its passengers a rough ride! Was Sydenham the name of the coach operator?

A Mother's Union outing to Teignmouth. It was paid for by a member who was resident in one of Teignmouth's hotels.

can be found in a book entitled *Cluster-o'-Vive* by Professor John Read F.R.S, published by the Somerset Folk Press in 1923. This book (No. 11 in the Somerset Folk series) contains true stories, as Professor Read was resident in Sparkford at one time. This and two other books by the same author are now very hard to find. The other two, *Latter-Lammas* and *Wold Ways Again* take the form of dialect plays and sketches. The rustic form of dialect in all three books represents a worthwhile attempt to preserve it and even those from outside this area will not find it too difficult to read and understand. The task is made easier by reference to the glossary of terms thoughtfully included by the author.

On 6th August 1954 a whirlwind hit Sparkford, described by onlookers as 'a towering black funnel that stretched up into the sky as high as you could see, revolving very slowly'. Following torrential rain, it swept through Donald Cluett's orchard at Manor Farm, tearing down several trees and leaving a trail of debris. In one of the cow sheds, Jack Meaker, a farm worker, found he could hardly keep his feet. The houses in Green Close suffered the most, especially the house occupied by Jim Toop, which had a gaping hole torn in its roof after 70 tiles had been ripped off. Such was the noise than many thought an aircraft had crashed near by. Although the whirlwind took only about a minute and a half to pass, it proved a terrifying time for many, who were afraid their house was about to fall in upon them. Yet it was a quite localised happening as all had remained calm in Mudford, only five miles away.

To celebrate the coronation of H.R.H. Queen Elizabeth II in 1953, every man serving in the armed forces who lived in Sparkford was sent a pocket knife. In the

At the Coronation Day Children's Fancy Dress Parade, Nancy Hallett and David March won the Up to Five Year's Prize as Bride and Bridegroom. Making the costumes must have been anything but easy, as cloth and clothing were still on ration.

village, festivities on the day included a children's sports day and fancy dress parade, followed by a tea at which they were presented with commemorative mugs by the Rev. and Mrs J. R. Bellyse. Many adults took the opportunity to watch the coronation ceremony on a television set in the Parish Hall, whilst in the evening they watched a comic cricket match. The following day the adults had their own celebrations in the form of a dance and a social evening. A clock was placed in the Parish Hall to serve as a permanent reminder of this joyous occasion.

Incidents Involving Aircraft

Nowadays aircraft regularly overfly Sparkford in considerable numbers, as did our own and enemy aircraft during World War 2, yet perhaps surprisingly there is only one apparently unrecorded incident within the Parish despite the close proximity of the naval airbase at Yeovilton and its satellite at Sigwells. This occurred when an aircraft crashed at Brooklands Farm, shortly after Harry Brain had moved a cow from the cowshed it hit.

An early incident worth recording occurred during 1913, when a Farman biplane of the Royal Flying Corps got into difficulties whilst flying over Sparkford when returning to its base on Salisbury Plain via Dorchester. At 2,000 feet the engine started to misfire badly then stopped altogether, leaving the pilot no alternative but to try to land safely somewhere between the village and Sherborne. The field on which he touched down was rough, such that the biplane turned a complete somersault as soon as its wheels contacted the ground. Fortunately the pilot, Lt. Burroughs, and his unnamed NCO passenger suffered only superficial injuries, despite the latter losing a great deal of blood due to a badly lacerated face. The aircraft itself was a complete wreck, with only its engine relatively intact. The site of the crash drew large crowds of sightseers, who promptly removed parts of the wreckage to take away as mementos!

During World War 2 a number of our own military aircraft were involved in accidents near to Sparkford or in villages around the Sparkford area, many of them Hurricanes based at Yeovilton. The nearest recorded accident relates to a Hurricane from Yeovilton that crashed in the grounds of Hazlegrove House on 21st May 1941, killing its pilot.

It is also worth recording that a Heinkel He111 was shot down by a night fighter and crashed at Corton Denham late at night on 8th May 1941. A Dornier Do217 suffered a similar fate on 15th May 1944 and crashed at Camel Cross in the early hours of that morning.

In the '50s, an aircraft caught fire and after the crew had baled out it crashed in a field at Weston Bampfylde.

Although there is still much air activity in and around the Sparkford area, especially from RNAS Yeovilton, it says much for the current level of air safety that there has been no further incident to report within the village or its immediate surrounds.

Sparkford Today

During the past couple of decades life in Sparkford has not changed to any marked extent. Indeed, the village is now much quieter with less traffic passing through its centre following the opening of the long-awaited bypass. Some infilling with new houses has taken place, but even this has not occurred to any significant extent.

It seems inevitable that Sparkford will at some time be subjected to further development. The village has already been singled out as a 'key site' for this purpose by the South Somerset District Council, under pressure from the government to provide additional housing to meet the projected increase in population. Fortunately it is unlikely to follow the previous plan for 600 houses on the south western fringe of the village, which had subsequently to be abandoned. A well co-ordinated campaign by the parishioners had shown it could not be sustained in the absence of a supporting infrastructure. However, as improvements to the A303 continue and access to London and the motorway network becomes even quicker and easier as a consequence, some form of requirement for additional houses seems bound to follow. That is, assuming the government's controversial estimate of requirements can be substantiated. The general feeling within the village is that if this comes about, it needs to be restricted to carefully controlled in-fill.

Sources of Reference

A History of the Bennett Family by Roderick Bennett, a privately-compiled and illustrated family history. (Extracts kindly provided by the Rev. Guy Bennett.)

Book 1 (Home), Book 2 (Bennett) and Book 3 (Moberly). Unpublished recollections by Miss Edith Mary Bennett, daughter of Henry Edward Bennett. (Kindly loaned by Mrs Diana Gordon Clark.)

Brochure for the sale of the Sparkford Hall Estate. Messrs Wainwrights & Heard. 17th December 1918. (Copies kindly loaned by Mrs Pam Hoare and Lady Sara Loram.)

Village Heritage Book. Compiled by Members of Sparkford Women's Institute in conjunction with the European Architectural Heritage Year, 1975. (Kindly loaned by Mrs Pam Hoare.)

Sparkford Today. Compiled by Members of Sparkford Women's Institute to commemorate the Women's Institute Golden Jubilee Year, 1965. (Kindly loaned by Mrs Pam Hoare.)

Sparkford. A pamphlet compiled by the Rev. Patrick Connor (Rector) in 1979.

Haynes: The First 25 Years by Jeff Clew. J. H. Haynes & Co. Ltd, 1985.

The Parish News – various issues.

The Sparkford Vale Harriers by Mrs R. Wood. The Hunts Association, c1949.

The Story of the Westbury to Weymouth Line by Derek Phillips. Oxford Publishing Co., 1994. (Copyright permission kindly given by Derek Phillips.)

The Sparkford Bypass. A brochure published by the MRM Partnership for the Department of Transport to commemorate the opening of the bypass in October 1989. (Kindly loaned by Mrs Helen Tracy.)

Kelly's Directories. 1875, 1889 and 1927.

Letter from Ivor P. Collis, County Archivist, The Somerset Record Office, dated 25th February 1970. A letter to Mr D. Cluett giving as much as is known of the early history of Manor Farm. (Copy kindly provided by Mr Donald Cluett.)

Local Studies Pack for the Parish of Sparkford. Somerset County Council Library Services.

Cluster-o'-Vive by Professor John Read. Somerset Folk Press, Montacute, c1923. (Copy kindly loaned by Mr Gordon Moore B.E.M.)

Book of newspaper press cuttings from 1893 to 1922 compiled by Edwin Dampier. (Kindly loaned by Mrs Ann Aldworth.)

Somerset at War 1939-1945 by Mac Hawkins. The Dovecote Press, 1988.

1903 Ordnance Survey Map kindly loaned by Mr A. J. Gunn. (Reproduced in part by kind permission of Ordnance Survey.)

Book of press cuttings from 1920 to 1936 (Kindly loaned by Mr David Wood.)

Minutes of Sparkford Parish Council Meetings. Somerset County Council Records Office, Taunton.

List of Buildings of Special Architectural or Historic Interest. Department of the Environment, 1986.

Minutes of the Sparkford Vale Co-Operative Dairy Society's Annual General Meetings, 1919-1938. Somerset County Council Records Office, Taunton.

Landworker, September 1989.

Somerset and West Magazine, October 1978.

Somersetshire Country Houses and Villages. Truman Press, 1931-2. Limited numbered print.

From Parson's Quarter to Purgatory: A History of North Cadbury, Woolston and Galhampton. S. W. Miller. Castle Cary Press, 1988.

Acknowledgements

My grateful thanks to each of the following who provided much appreciated help by either talking to me about bygone times, lending me photographs to get copied, or books of press cuttings. Without their help the publication of this book would not have been possible.

Mrs Ann Aldworth.
Mrs Kay Baker.
The Rev. Guy Bennett.
Mr Robert Bennett.
Mr Tom Binding.
Mr Colin Caddy.
Castle Cary Public Library.
Mrs Diana Gordon Clark.
Mr Donald Cluett.
Mr Roger Giles.
Mr A. J. 'Ben' Gunn.
Mr John Haynes O.B.E.
Mrs Pam Hoare.
Mr Tony Hill.
Miss Ester Jenkins.
Mr and Mrs David King-Brain.
Lady Sara Loram.
Mrs Rose March.

Mr Gordon Moore B.E.M.
Ordnance Survey.
Mr Derek Phillips.
Mrs Freda Pittard.
Mrs M. Raynor.
Somerset County Council Records Office, Taunton.
Somerset Studies Library, Taunton.
Mr Morley Spencer.
Mr Jack Sugg.
Mr Jim Toop.
Mr Norman Toop.
Mrs Helen Tracy.
Mr Fred Warren.
Mrs Ros White.
Mr Jim Windsor.
Mr David Wood.
Mrs Betty Yeates.

Index

Tailpiece. Someone from South Barrow had a splendid sense of humour during the heavy snowfall of the winter of 1977/8!

The DReAm

Terry **LaBan**
Peter **Hogan**
Alisa **Kwitney**
WRITERS

Peter **Snejbjerg**
Steve **Parkhouse**
Michael **Zulli**
Dick **Giordano**
ARTISTS

Daniel **Vozzo**
COLORIST & SEPARATOR

Todd **Klein**
Steve **Parkhouse**
Annie **Parkhouse**
LETTERERS

Dave **McKean**
COVERS

Neil **Gaiman**
CONSULTANT

Peter **Hogan**
Joe **Orlando**
INTRODUCTION

THE DREAMING created by *Neil* **Gaiman**

BeyonD the SHores of Night

THE DREAMING: BEYOND THE SHORES OF NIGHT
ISBN 1 85286 904 6
Published by Titan Books, Ltd, 42-44 Dolben St., London SE1 0UP
under licence from DC Comics. Cover, introduction and compilation
copyright © 1998 DC Comics. All Rights Reserved.

Originally published in single magazine form as THE DREAMING 1-8.
Copyright © 1996, 1997 DC Comics. All Rights Reserved. VERTIGO and all
characters, their distinctive likenesses and related indicia featured in this
publication are trademarks of DC Comics. The stories, characters, and incidents
featured in this publication are entirely fictional. Printed in Canada

10 9 8 7 6 5 4 3 2 1

First Edition: January 1998
To order titles from the backlist page, please quote reference code DR/GN.

Cover by *Dave* **McKean**
Publication design by *Murphy* **Fogelnest**

The Goldie Factor

ABEL, MY BROTHER, I MUST TELL YOU FRANKLY-- YOU DON'T APPEAR TO BE AT YOUR BEST THIS EVENING.

I-I DUH*DON'T*? I FUH*FEEL* ALL RIGHT.

THAT'S WHAT I *MEAN*. YOU'RE SO PINK-CHEEKED AND JOLLY, BRIMMING WITH LIFE, I THINK YOU'D LOOK *MUCH* BETTER WITH YOUR HEAD SMASHED IN, OR WITH A HUNTING KNIFE BURIED IN YOUR AMPLE GUT.

BUHBUHBUHBUT CAIN... I HUHHAVEN'T TUHTOLD ANY SECRETS OR REVEALED ANY MUH*MYSTERIES*...

TSK, ABEL--IT DISTRESSES ME TO SEE YOU BECOMING SUCH A HIDEBOUND OLD FUDDY-DUDDY. WE DON'T *ALWAYS* HAVE TO HAVE A REASON.

WHUMP!

≥HOOF!≤

CUH*CAIN*... PLEASE...

CAIN... NO...

SHICK!

THE GOLDIE FACTOR
PART ONE

TERRY LaBAN, writer • PETER SNEJBJERG, artist
DANIEL VOZZO, colorist & separator
TODD KLEIN, letterer • ALISA KWITNEY, editor
NEIL GAIMAN, consultant

The Dreaming created by
NEIL GAIMAN

awk!

OOOOOOH....

OOOOH...
OH MY...

GUHGUH-
GOLDIE?

Meep.

GOLDIE! AND
GUHGREGORY TOO!
WHY, THUH *THANK*
YOU!

UMM!
≳SMACK!≲
RUHRUHOAST LOIN OF BUHBUHBASILISK! MY FUHFAVORITE!

er... HAS GREGORY BEEN HERE ALL ALUH-LOHLONG?

WELL, MUHMAYBE HE OUGHT TO GO HOME NOW. CUHCAIN MIGHT COME LUH LOOKING FOR HIM.

YUHYUH-YOU CUHCAN SEE HIM LATER, GUHGOLDIE.

Meep!

OH. THUHTHAT ISN'T IT?

≳Sigh≲ ...GUHGOLDIE... IT'S NUH NOT THAT BAD. I'M USED TO IT NOW.

ANYWUHWAY, AFTER HE'S DUHDONE IT, HE USUALLY LUHLEAVES ME ALONE FOR A FUHFEW DUHDAYS.

OH, GOLDIE! DHUHDON'T BE MAD! THUH-THUHTHUH...

...THUHTHERE'S A LOT YOU SUHSTILL DUHDON'T UNDER-STAND.

GOLDIE!

12

GREGORY! I'VE BEEN LOOKING ALL **OVER** FOR YOU.

KICK!

YOU KNOW, GREGORY, YOU OUGHT TO TRY MAKING YOURSELF A LITTLE MORE AVAILABLE, IT'S GETTING PRETTY TIRESOME WEARING OUT A PAIR OF BOOTS EVERY TIME I WANT TO FIND YOU.

COME ALONG NOW!

AWRK?

EH? OF **COURSE** GOLDIE CAN COME, IF SHE WISHES. HOW ABOUT IT, GOLDIE? I'LL BET AN HOUR OR TWO AT THE HOUSE OF MYSTERY WOULD BE A WELCOME RESPITE FROM THE TIRESOME COMPANY OF THAT HALF-WIT I CALL "BROTHER!"

HEY!

PTOO!

WHY... WHY, YOU MISERABLE LITTLE NEWTLING! WHY'D YOU DO THAT?!

BLESS MY BEARD! IT REALLY...

PSsssssSs

...HURTS!

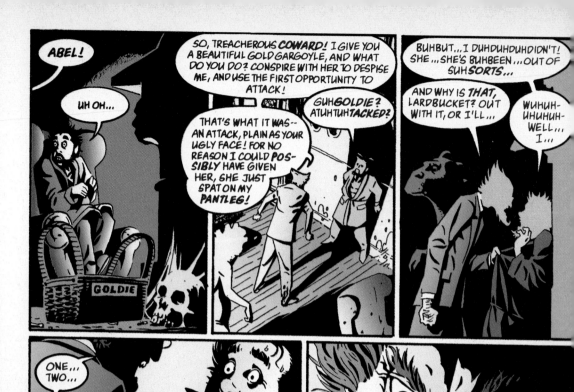

ABEL!

UH OH...

GOLDIE

SO, TREACHEROUS **COWARD!** I GIVE YOU A BEAUTIFUL GOLD GARGOYLE, AND WHAT DO YOU DO? CONSPIRE WITH HER TO DESPISE ME, AND USE THE FIRST OPPORTUNITY TO ATTACK!

GUH**GOLDIE**? ATUHTUH**TACKED**?

THAT'S WHAT IT WAS-- AN ATTACK, PLAIN AS YOUR UGLY FACE! FOR NO REASON I COULD POSSIBLY HAVE GIVEN HER, SHE JUST SPAT ON MY **PANTLEG!**

BUHBUT... I DUHDUHDUHDIDN'T! SHE...SHE'S BUHBEEN...OUT OF SUH**SORTS**...

AND WHY IS **THAT**, LARDBUCKET? OUT WITH IT, OR I'LL...

WUHUH-UHUHUH-WELL... I...

ONE... TWO...

I...I DUHDUHDON'T THINK SHE LUHLIKES THE WAY YOU TUH**TREAT** ME!

DOESN'T LIKE THE WAY I...

awk!

WELL, SPEAK OF THE DEVIL, OR THE GARGOYLE, AS IT WERE. SO, GOLDIE-- I HAVE IT ON **GOOD** AUTHORITY YOU'RE TROUBLED BY THE WAY I'M **RUNNING** THINGS HERE.

I'M SORRY TO HEAR YOU HAVE A COMPLAINT. BUT I **DO** WISH YOU'D FOUND A MORE AGREEABLE WAY TO BRING IT TO MY ATTENTION.

OH!

YOU SEE, WE'RE A **FAMILY**, AND IT'S IMPORTANT THAT WE HAVE THE PROPER **REGARD** FOR EACH OTHER. AM I RIGHT, BROTHER?

CUH-CUH-CUH-CUH...

YOU HEAR, GOLDIE? ABEL AGREES.

OF COURSE, HE MIGHT NOT PUT IT QUITE THAT WAY. AS YOU KNOW, ABEL'S A MAN OF FEW WORDS, HE PREFERS TO SET AN EXAMPLE.

ASK HIM WHEN HE GETS BETTER AGAIN, AND I'M SURE HE'LL EXPLAIN...

...THAT YOU REALLY SHOULDN'T GET ALL HOT AND BOTHERED JUST BECAUSE WE OCCASION-ALLY DO...

...THIS!

WHUMP!

HEY!

BAD IDEA, GOLDIE!

HATE ME IF YOU WANT TO, BUT INTERFERE WITH ME, AND I'LL...

GRRRR RRRRR!

UMM! WHUHWHUHWHAT'S THAT SUHSMELL?

GOLDIE! GOLDIE, DID YOU MUHMAKE BREAKFAST ALREADY?

YUM! DUH-DORMOUSE OMELETTE!

BUT, WUHWHY DID SHE *LEAVE* IT LIKE THUH-THIS?

GOLDIE?

GOLD-EE!

GOLDIE? GOLD... WHUWHUWHU....

OH NUHNUHNO! SHE CUH *COULDN'T* HAVE!

18

WUHWHERE DO YOU THINK SHE COULD *BE*?

I WISH YOU'D STOP *ASKING* ME THAT. IF SHE WERE IN THE PLACES I *THOUGHT* SHE'D BE, WE WOULD'VE *FOUND* HER BY NOW.

I NUHNEVER THOUGHT SHE'D ACTUALLY *LEAVE* US. GREGORY'S HUHARDLY EVER EVEN BEEN OUT OF *SIGHT*!

THAT'S NO SURPRISE. GREGORY'S A *REGULAR* GARGOYLE.

HUHHOW'S THAT DUHDIFFERENT?

GOLDIE'S A *GOLDEN* GARGOYLE.

I *KNOW*, CUHCAIN. THUH-THAT'S HER COLOR.

WELL, *OBVIOUSLY*, IT'S MORE THAN *THAT*! IT'S WELL-KNOWN BY ALL BUT THE FAT AND STUPID THAT GOLDEN GARGOYLES ARE...

THEY CAN...

UM...

WELL, I'M NOT PRECISELY SURE.

A-ARE YOU SUHSAY-ING IT'S A *MYSTERY*? I THOUGHT YOU KNEW TH-THE SOLUTION TO ALL MUHMYSTERIES.

AS A MATTER OF *FACT*, BLUBBERBUTT, IT'S A *SECRET*. SO *YOU'RE* THE ONE WHO OUGHT TO KNOW IT!

BUHBUHBUT I *DON'T*! I DIDN'T EVEN KNOW THERE *WERE* GOLDEN GARGOYLES TILL THAT EGG YOU GUHGAVE ME *HATCHED*!

CAIN...WHERE DID YOU *GET* THUHTHAT EGG, ANYWAY?

I....BOUGHT IT.

20

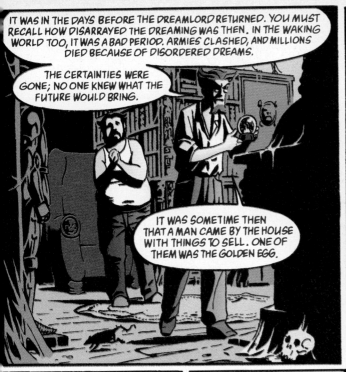

IT WAS IN THE DAYS BEFORE THE DREAMLORD RETURNED. YOU MUST RECALL HOW DISARRAYED THE DREAMING WAS THEN. IN THE WAKING WORLD TOO, IT WAS A BAD PERIOD. ARMIES CLASHED, AND MILLIONS DIED BECAUSE OF DISORDERED DREAMS.

THE CERTAINTIES WERE GONE; NO ONE KNEW WHAT THE FUTURE WOULD BRING.

IT WAS SOMETIME THEN THAT A MAN CAME BY THE HOUSE WITH THINGS TO SELL. ONE OF THEM WAS THE GOLDEN EGG.

WHEN I SAW IT, I IMMEDIATELY WANTED IT. HE TOLD ME IT WAS VALUABLE AND RARE, AND SAID NEVER TO LET IT OUT OF MY SIGHT.

AND YET, IT WAS SURPRISINGLY CHEAP. A COUPLE OF MINOR ENIGMAS, I THINK, NOTHING I HAD TO STOP AND CONSIDER. HE WANTED TO GET RID OF IT, I SUPPOSE.

DUHDID YOU ASK WHUWHERE *HE* GOT IT?

NO. THERE WERE A LOT OF THINGS... AVAILABLE IN THOSE DAYS. I DIDN'T WANT TO FRIGHTEN HIM OFF.

WUHWAS IT *STOLEN?*

I *TOLD* YOU, YOU THICK TWIT, I DON'T KNOW! ANYWAY, I DIDN'T CARE. I JUST WANTED IT.

BUHBUT CAIN... IF YOU WUHWUH-WANTED IT SO MUCH... WHY DUHDID YOU GIVE IT TO...

...MUH-MUHMUHMUH-*ME?*

I... I HADN'T INTENDED TO, BUT THE EGG... IT WAS AS IF THE EGG *ITSELF* HAD A WILL OF ITS OWN. IT *WANTED* ME TO GIVE IT TO YOU, AND IT WAS VERY... *PERSUASIVE.*

WUHWUHWUHWE REALLY DON'T KNUHKNOW *ANYTHING* ABOUT GOLDIE, DO WE?

NO. I SUPPOSE WE DON'T.

MUHMAYBE WE OUGHT TO GO TO THE LUHLIBRARY. I BET LUHLUCIEN CAN HELP US.

LUCIEN? IT'S JUST LIKE YOU, YOU SPONGE-WITTED GOLLIWOG, TO WANT TO GO BOTHERING WITH THAT STARCHY, WORM-EATEN BORE OF A LIBRARI...

HMM. EVERY ONCE IN A WHILE, BROTHER, YOU MAKE A SUGGESTION THAT ISN'T WORTHLESS.

PERHAPS SOME RESEARCH IN THE ARCHIVES *WOULD* PROVE USEFUL. IT'S A PLACE TO START, ANYHOW.

BUT I HAVE AN INKLING IT'D BE BEST NOT TO GO ADVERTISING THE FACT THAT WE'VE LOST GOLDIE. LET *ME* DO THE TALKING, UNDERSTAND?

OW! A-A-A-ALL *RIGHT!*

GOLDEN GARGOYLES, EH? WHY, THAT'S QUITE NOVEL, YOU KNOW. WE GET VERY FEW INQUIRIES ABOUT GOLDEN GARGOYLES, ONLY ONE THAT I RECALL.

HOW *FASCINATING*, LUCIEN. WE'VE ONLY BEEN HERE TEN MINUTES, AND ALREADY WE'RE *OVERWHELMED* WITH USEFUL INFORMATION.

I ONLY REMEMBER IT BECAUSE THE CHAP WAS QUITE UNUSUAL, IN THAT HE HAD NO ARMS OR LEGS. QUITE LIMBLESS, AS IT WERE.

PERHAPS YOU KNOW HIM--I DOUBT THERE ARE MANY WHO SHARE AN INTEREST IN GARGOYLES OF THE GILDED VARIETY.

I'LL BET THERE ARE FEWER WHO CAN TOLERATE YOUR WITLESS CHATTER FOR MORE THAN HALF A MINUTE AT A TIME. HOW MUCH MORE OF IT WILL *WE* HAVE TO STAND BEFORE YOU *HELP* US?

EXCUSE ME, BUT THERE'S NO REASON FOR THAT SORT OF TONE. I FIND A PLEASANT ATTITUDE MAKES THINGS GO EASIER ALL AROUND.

GOLDEN GARGOYLES, PLEASE!

WE DO HAVE SOMETHING, BUT I'M NOT SURE HOW MUCH. AS I SAID, IT'S QUITE AN OBSCURE TOPIC.

HMMM. WELL, HERE'S WHAT THERE IS. GARGOYLES, OF COURSE, GUARD THINGS, USUALLY PLACES WHERE MYSTERIES AND SECRETS ARE EXPLORED OR CELEBRATED. CHURCHES, UNIVERSITIES...

OR OUR HUHOUSES!

QUITE SO. THAT'S WHY YOU HAVE SO MANY. NOW, GOLDEN GARGOYLES DO THE SAME SORT OF THING, BUT, AS THEY SAY, MORE SO.

WHAT'S *THAT* MEAN?

JUST THAT THEY'RE MUCH MORE POWERFUL, I SUPPOSE. IT DOESN'T SAY ANY MORE THAN THAT, AT LEAST NOT HERE.

WAIT... THIS IS ODD.

SOMEONE'S RIPPED THE NEXT FEW PAGES OUT OF THIS BOOK! IT'S TERRIBLE! WHO'D DO SOMETHING LIKE THAT?

22

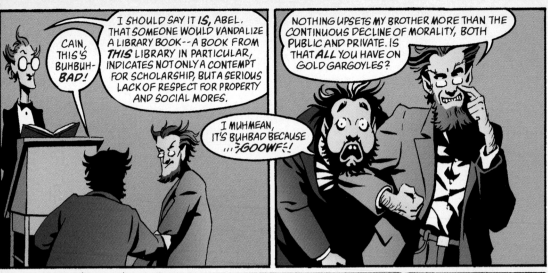

23

BUT CUHCAIN... WHY DOES IT HAVE TO BE SUCH A SUH- *SECRET?*

A BETTER QUESTION IS WHY *SHOULDN'T* IT BE? YOU, OF ALL PEOPLE, OUGHT TO KNOW *THAT.* IF THAT POINTY-HEADED STUFFSHIRT DOESN'T KNOW ENOUGH TO HELP US, WE OUGHT TO AT LEAST MAKE SURE HE DOESN'T KNOW ENOUGH TO *HURT* US.

BUT MAYBE HE *COULD* HELP US, IF WE TUHTOLD HIM MORE.

HE COULD HELP US WASTE ANY TIME WE HAD TO SPARE, BUT SINCE WE *DON'T* HAVE ANY, HIS USEFULNESS IS NIL.

THERE MUST BE SOMEONE ELSE AROUND HERE WHO WE CAN ASK ABOUT GOLDEN GARGOYLES, SOMEONE WITH SOME KNOWLEDGE OF THE DREAMING THAT DOESN'T DEPEND ON A HANDFUL OF WORM-EATEN PARCHMENT PAGES.

WHAT ABOUT E-EVE?

EVE? OH, PLEASE --WE'D FIND OUT MORE BY SLICING OPEN YOUR STOMACH AND READING YOUR GUTS LIKE AN ORACLE THAN CRAWLING UP TO THAT LOATHSOME CAVE AND LISTEN-ING TO EVE SPOUT HER CRYPTIC...

THE WAITRESS WILL SEAT YOU

EVE! OF COURSE! SHE'S BEEN HERE SINCE THE BEGINNING AND SHE KNOWS MORE ABOUT THE DREAMING THAN ANYONE. PLUS, SHE WON'T BLAB OUR BUSINESS FROM EVERY HILL AND DALE.

COME ALONG, LUMPKIN--LET'S PAY A VISIT TO EVE.

LISTEN, ALAN, YOU'LL HAVE TO EXCUSE ME, BUT SOMETHING'S JUST COME UP.

BUT...YOU CAN'T JUST *LEAVE* ME LIKE THIS! YOU WERE GIVING ME *ADVICE!*

WHAT ELSE CAN I TELL YOU, HMMM? JUST GO FOR IT. IT'S YOUR WIFE'S OWN FAULT FOR BEING A *FRIGID BITCH.*

BUT...

COME ON, ALAN--LET'S *DO* IT! RIGHT HERE ON THE *TABLE!*

HELLO THERE! MIND IF I JOIN YOU?

awk.

ALLOW ME TO INTRODUCE MYSELF. I'M KNOWN, HERE AND ABROAD, AS TEMPTO THE INTUITOR. A BIT DRAMATIC, I SUPPOSE, BUT YOU NEED A LITTLE DRAMA TO GET PEOPLE'S ATTENTION.

LIKE SOME COFFEE?

WAITER, COFFEE OVER HERE!

ANYHOW, THOUGH AS YOU CAN SEE, MY PHYSICAL MOBILITY IS LIMITED, MY *MIND* HAS THE POWER TO ROAM THE SOULS OF MEN. OR GARGOYLES, AS IT WERE. YOU, FOR INSTANCE. I HAVE AN INKLING ABOUT YOU. IT'S GETTING CLEARER... YES! YOUR NAME IS GOLDIE! AM I RIGHT?

Awk?

HOW DID I KNOW? DON'T ASK-- I DON'T KNOW MYSELF. IT'S JUST A TALENT. A SMALL THING, PERHAPS, BUT IT HELPS ME MAKE MY WAY IN THE WORLD. WE HAVE TO WORK WITH WHAT WE HAVE, HMMM?

YOU STRIKE ME AS BEING TALENTED YOURSELF, GOLDIE. HAVE YOU ANY TALENTS?

OH, I'LL BET YOU DO. YOU PROBABLY JUST DON'T *KNOW* ABOUT THEM YET, HMMMM?

SO, GOLDIE, WHAT BRINGS YOU TO THE OLD LABYRINTH THIS EVENING? JUST CRAVING A CUP OF JAVA AND SOME PIE?

HMMM. THERE'S SOMETHING MORE, ISN'T THERE? I'M GETTING AN IMAGE HERE...PAIN, VIOLENCE. A PROBLEM AT HOME, AM I RIGHT?

meep!

OH, DEAR. SORE POINT, HMMM? THERE, THERE. LET IT ALL OUT. IT'S NOT YOU, BUT SOMEONE YOU LOVE VERY MUCH. YES. I CAN SEE.

MY, MY. IT MUST BE TERRIBLE, IT REALLY MUST. HAVE A LITTLE COFFEE--THERE YOU GO.

I DON'T BLAME YOU FOR LEAVING. NOT A BIT.

SO, WHAT NOW? NO PLANS, EH? WELL, THAT'S NOT BAD. MAKE A FRESH START, AND DON'T GIVE A SECOND *THOUGHT* TO ALL THAT BACK THERE. YOU TRIED YOUR BEST, DIDN'T YOU? YOU *CAN'T* HELP ANYONE WHO DOESN'T WANT TO HELP THEMSELVES.

Meep!

OH MY! THERE YOU GO AGAIN. YOU MUST CARE FOR YOUR FRIEND VERY MUCH.

LISTEN, GOLDIE...

ORDINARILY, I DON'T GET INVOLVED WITH THE PROBLEMS OF THE PEOPLE I COUNSEL, BUT FOR SOME REASON, I REALLY *LIKE* YOU.

I CAN'T TELL YOU WHY. IT'S JUST A FEELING. BUT, AS YOU'VE SEEN, MY FEELINGS ARE USUALLY WORTH TRUSTING. HMMM?

LET ME ASK YOU A QUESTION, ALL RIGHT? LET'S JUST SAY, FOR PURPOSES OF DISCUSSION, THAT THERE WAS A WAY FOR YOU TO HELP YOUR FRIEND. WOULD YOU DO IT?

Meep.

OF *COURSE!* OF *COURSE* YOU WOULD!

BUT WHAT IF IT REQUIRED A DANGEROUS, UNCOMFORTABLE JOURNEY TO THE WILDEST, MOST OBSCURE PART OF THE DREAMING. WOULD YOU *STILL* DO IT?

Meep.

EVEN IF THERE WAS A GOOD CHANCE YOU *YOURSELF* MIGHT NOT COME BACK?

Meep! Meep!

WELL, I MUST SAY I'M IMPRESSED. THIS FRIEND OF YOURS IS AWFULLY LUCKY.

HMMM. I THINK WE OUGHT TO TALK, GOLDIE. I REALLY DO.

BUT WHY NOT HAVE A BITE TO EAT FIRST? THE HOT MANTICORE LOAF ISN'T BAD, AND OF COURSE, YOU CAN'T GO WRONG WITH A BURGER. GO ON, KNOCK YOURSELF OUT. IT'S MY TREAT.

WHATCHA DOIN', EVE?

NOTHING.

WANNA PLAY A GAME? WHY DON'TCHA THROW SOME BREAD SO I CAN CATCH IT IN MY BEAK?

NO. I DON'T FEEL LIKE IT.

WHY? IS SOMETHING WRONG?

I HAD A DREAM.

A DREAM? HOW DOES THAT WORK? YOU'RE ALREADY IN THE DREAMING.

I KNOW. I HAD ONE ANYWAY.

SO-- WHAT WAS IT?

I SAW SOMEONE I KNEW A LONG TIME AGO.

WHO?

JUST SOMEONE. HE WAS MEAN TO ME.

IN THE DREAM?

NO. HE DIDN'T DO ANYTHING IN THE DREAM. EXCEPT LOOK AT ME.

IT BOTHERED ME. I HAVEN'T SEEN HIM FOR A LONG TIME.

OH WELL. IT'S JUST A DREAM, RIGHT?

I GUESS SO.

EVE! OH, EVE! YOO HOO!

NOTHING THAT'LL CAUSE MAJOR INCONVENIENCE, DEAR. WE'D JUST LIKE TO ASK YOU A QUESTION OR TWO, AND THEN WE'LL BE ON OUR WAY.

IT'LL JUST TAKE A MOMENT, I'M SURE. WE ONLY WANT TO FIND OUT WHAT YOU KNOW ABOUT GOLDEN GARGOYLES.

I'D RATHER NOT ANSWER QUESTIONS NOW. I'D RATHER PEOPLE NOT DISTURB ME AT ALL.

THAT'S WHY YOU'VE COME? MOST PEOPLE WHO WANTED THAT SORT OF INFORMATION WOULD GO TO THE LIBRARY.

RIGHT YOU ARE! THAT WAS OUR VERY FIRST STOP. BUT LUCIEN COULDN'T TELL US ANYTHING, AND THE PAGES WERE MISSING FROM THE ONLY BOOK THAT MENTIONED THE SUBJECT.

IT'S NOT IMPORTANT TO ME. AND NOW, SINCE WE HAVE NOTHING MORE TO SAY TO EACH OTHER, I'D APPRECIATE IT IF YOU'D LEAVE.

BUHBUT EVE... WUHWE LOST GOLDIE!

EVE! GREETINGS AND SALUTATIONS! SORRY TO BARGE IN ON YOU LIKE THIS, BUT THERE DIDN'T SEEM TO BE ANY REASONABLE WAY OF CALLING AHEAD.

CAIN AND ABEL! WHAT ARE YOU DOING HERE?

PLEASE, EVE, CAN'T YOU HELP US? IT'S VERY IMPORTANT.

YOU LOST GOLDIE?

IT...IT'S TRUE, EVE. GOLDIE RAN AWAY, AND WE HAVE NO IDEA HOW TO FIND HER. AS I SAID, WE SPOKE TO LUCIEN, BUT HE WAS USELESS.

HE TOLD YOU NOTHING AT ALL?

ONLY THAT GOLD GARGOYLES WERE IMPORTANT IN SOME WAY. MORE IMPORTANT THAN RUN-OF-THE-MILL GARGOYLES, ANYHOW. BUT THAT MUCH WE'D ALREADY SURMISED.

OH! HE SUHSAID THE ONLY OTHER PERSON WHO'D EVER A-ASKED ABOUT THEM...

...HUHHUHHAD NO ARMS OR LEGS.

OH, I'M SURE THAT'S A CRUCIAL ELEMENT! HONESTLY, ABEL, YOUR CAPACITY TO ABSORB THE USELESS AND THE IRRELEVANT NEVER CEASES TO ASTOUND ME!

WAIT, CAIN. I DON'T KNOW HOW MUCH I CAN TELL YOU ABOUT GOLDEN GARGOYLES...

...BUT MY LIFE WAS RUINED FOREVER BY AN ARMLESS, LEGLESS MAN.

GODDAMNIT, THAT LITTLE FUCKER STIFFED ME AGAIN!

To Be Continued...

the DREAMING

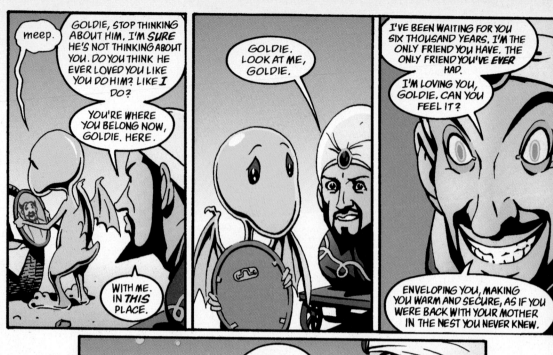

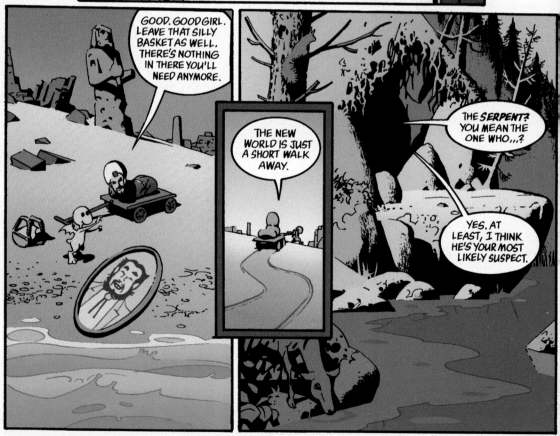

I'M SURE I DON'T HAVE TO TELL YOU THAT THE DREAMING ISN'T EXACTLY CROWDED WITH LIMBLESS MEN.

BUT HE'S NOT EXACTLY *OBSCURE*, IS HE? WOULDN'T LUCIEN HAVE *KNOWN* HIM?

MAYBE NOT. HE CAN CONCEAL HIS IDENTITY BY MANIPULATING THE PERCEPTIONS OF OTHERS. HE'S CURSED, CAIN, AS YOU ARE, BUT WITHOUT YOUR PROTECTION.

STILL, HIS RUSES LARGELY DEPEND ON THE FACT THAT NO ONE'S LOOKING FOR HIM TO BEGIN WITH. IF YOU WERE, HE PROBABLY WOULDN'T BE HARD TO FIND.

BUT WHY WOULD HE BE INTERESTED IN GOLD GARGOYLES?

THAT YOU'D HAVE TO ASK *HIM*.

BUT I REALLY WOULDN'T BOTHER. HE'S THE ORIGINAL PATHOLOGICAL LIAR.

I'D STILL LIKE TO GIVE IT A TRY. WE COULDN'T BE WORSE OFF THAN WE ARE NOW.

I WOULDN'T ASSUME THAT, CAIN. IF HE FINDS OUT GOLDIE IS LOST, HE COULD POSE A SERIOUS DANGER TO HER. I WOULDN'T BE SURPRISED IF HE ALREADY *DOES*.

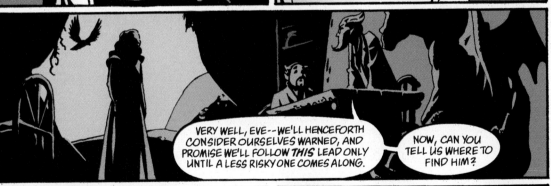

VERY WELL, EVE-- WE'LL HENCEFORTH CONSIDER OURSELVES WARNED, AND PROMISE WE'LL FOLLOW *THIS* LEAD ONLY UNTIL A LESS RISKY ONE COMES ALONG.

NOW, CAN YOU TELL US WHERE TO FIND HIM?

I'VE HEARD HE REGULARLY SPENDS TIME AT THE LABYRINTH GRILL, IN THE DREAMING VILLAGE. APPARENTLY HE AMUSES HIMSELF BY TEMPTING DREAMERS WITH THINGS FORBIDDEN THEM IN THEIR WAKING LIFE. YOU MIGHT CHECK FOR HIM THERE.

THUTHAT WOULD BE A GUHGOOD PLACE TO START. I COULD GUHGET A HUH- *HAMBURGER.*

OH, NO-- YOU'RE NOT STARTING IN ON THE HAMBURGERS. BY THE TIME YOU'RE DONE STUFFING GROUND MEAT INTO YOUR CAPACIOUS MAW, GOLDIE WILL BE *LIGHT* YEARS AWAY FROM HERE.

DUHDUHDUHDON'T WORRY, CUHCAIN. I'LL GUHGET IT TO GO.

CAIN, ABEL-- PLEASE. YOU MUST BE CAREFUL.

HE MAY ONLY BE A SHADOW OF WHAT HE WAS, BUT STILL, IF THERE'S ANY WAY HE CAN HURT YOU, HE WILL.

FOR NO OTHER REASON BUT THE SPITE OF IT, AND WITH NO THOUGHT FOR WHETHER OR NOT...

...HE HURTS HIMSELF.

MAN WEET NO ARMS OR LEGS. YEAH, WE GOTTA GUY LIKE DAT HANG AROUND HERE.

HEY, YOU WANT KETCHUP AN MUSTARD WIT'DOSE, RIGHT?

FINE GREEK SPECIAL

ALWAYS OPEN

YUH-YUHYUH-YEAH!

WE MAKE A GOOD BORGER, NO? EVERYONE COME FOR DAT. DAT AN' DA AMBROSIA OMELETTE. YOU TRIED DUH OMELETTE?

UH HUH.

GOOD, UH? HEY, YOU WANT MORE COFFEE?

I ASSURE YOU, MY BROTHER ISN'T SHY ABOUT EXTOLLING THE MERITS OF YOUR BURGERS WHEREVER HE GOES. NOW, WOULD YOU PLEASE FINISH TELLING US ABOUT THIS MAN?

LIKE I TOL' YOU, HE'S HERE ALL DA TIME.

SO WHERE IS HE NOW?

NOW, HE'S NOT HERE. IN FACT, I DON' THINK I SEEN HIM SINCE YESTERDAY.

I ASK DA WAITRESS, OKAY? LOOK, YOU SURE YOU GOT NO TIME TO EAT? IN THE TIME YOU BEEN HERE ALREADY, YOU COULDA HAD A BOWL A SOUP, AT LEAST.

AWRIGHT-- BE HONGRY, DEN.

HEY, ANIKA-- YOU SEEN DAT LITTLE REGULAR WIT NO ARMS OR LEGS?

YOU MEAN TEMPTO? LISTEN, IF I DO SEE HIS CHEAP ASS IN HERE AGAIN, I'LL PERSONALLY KICK IT OUT THE DOOR!

HEY, HEY, WATCH DA LANGUAGE! I DON' LIKE DAT ON DA FLOOR.

I'M SORRY, GUS, BUT YESTERDAY HE STIFFED ME AGAIN. IN THE CENTURY OR SO HE'S BEEN COMIN' HERE, I DON'T THINK HE'S TIPPED ME ONCE!

AW, C'MON, ANIKA, ALL HE EVER *HAS* IS COFFEE.

MISS-- EXCUSE ME!

NOT YESTERDAY. YESTERDAY HE SITS IN A BOOTH FOR *HOURS* WITH A SHINY LITTLE GARGOYLE, THEY BOTH HAVE A DINNER SPECIAL, COFFEE AND DESSERT, AND HE LEAVES ME EXACT *CHANGE!*

NO, WAIT-- IT WAS FIVE CENTS *SHORT!*

AWRIGHT, SO HE'S A BASTARD. STILL, HE'S A CUSTOMER, AND YOU GOTTA...

DID YOU SAY HE WAS WITH A GOLD GARGOYLE?

YEAH, THAT'S RIGHT. A CUTE LITTLE THING, CARRYING A BASKET. THEY SAT THERE FOR ABOUT THREE HOURS, HAPPY AS CAN BE, AN' THEN THEY STIFFED ME.

DID THEY LEAVE TOGETHER?

YEAH, I THINK SO.

WHERE WERE THEY GOING? DO YOU HAVE ANY IDEA?

NO WAY, MISTER. THE LESS I KNOW ABOUT TEMPTO THE BETTER. IN HERE ALL THE TIME, DOIN' SOME KINDA WEIRD BUSINESS WITH THE CUSTOMERS--HE GIVES ME THE CREEPS, Y'KNOW? PLUS, HE'S UGLIER THAN A TROLL'S REAR END.

MFR!

GREAT PILES OF ROTTING WEREWOLF THIGHS! GOLDIE'S BEEN KIDNAPPED BY THE VERY *ARCHITECT* OF ORIGINAL SIN!

WELL, *THIS* IS A FINE PICKLE! WHAT ARE WE GOING TO DO? WE DON'T EVEN KNOW WHICH *DOOR* THEY WENT OUT OF.

I'LL BUHBUHBET GUHGREGORY COULD FUHFIND IT.

OH, YES, GREGORY. AND WHAT DO YOU SUPPOSE *HE'LL* DO, YOU SAD REJECT FROM A DOG FOOD FACTORY? JUST *TRACK* GOLDIE ACROSS THE DREAMING LIKE SOME B-MOVIE PRISON WARDEN'S BLOOD...

SAY! YOU MIGHT HAVE SOMETHING THERE-- GREGORY'S GOT A NOSE THAT ANY HOUND WOULD PAY DEARLY TO OWN.

BUT THERE'S STILL A SLIGHT HITCH-- WE DON'T HAVE ANYTHING WITH GOLDIE'S SCENT.

WHUWHAT ABOUT THE PUHPUHPLACE SHE WAS SUH*SITTING*?

GOOD GUESS, EINSTEIN, BUT THERE'S PROBABLY BEEN *DOZENS* OF ODIFEROUS BEHINDS IN THAT SEAT SINCE SHE LEFT.

WAIT A SECOND, YOU GUYS. I JUST REMEMBERED --THAT LITTLE THING WASN'T SITTING RIGHT ON THE BOOTH SEAT.

I DON'T THINK ANYTHING'S SAT IN IT SINCE HER. WE HAVEN'T HAD MUCH SMALL TRAFFIC LATELY. JUST SOME PIXIES THIS MORNING, BUT THEY ALL SAT ON SUGAR PACKETS.

SNF? SNF?

C'MON, FATSO! HE'S ON TO SOMETHING!

HEY! WAIT A MINUTE!

DAMN IT! DOESN'T *ANYONE* TIP ANYMORE?

HOW ABOUT IT, GREGORY? SMELL GOLDIE ANYWHERE?

ROORT.

YOU CAN'T SMELL *ANYTHING* IN THIS PLACE-- IT'S TOO DAMN *STERILE*.

I DUHDON'T THINK GOLDIE WOULD LUH-LIKE IT HERE.

THEN LET'S TAKE THESE SHARES AND TRADE 'EM FOR SOMETHING MORE LIKELY, BEFORE WE GET RUN OVER BY A HOVER-CRAFT.

WELL, SHE'S NOT IN THE WORKER'S PARADISE.

OR IN ECOTOPIA.

OR IN NORMAN ROCKWELL'S AMERICA.

BAH! I'VE HAD IT WITH THESE PIE-IN-THE-SKY COLLECTIVE DELUSIONS OF THE GOOD LIFE!

BUHBUT *GOLDIE* MIGHT LIKE THEM.

IF SHE WAS THERE, WE WOULD HAVE SEEN HER. THERE'S NOWHERE TO HIDE IN THESE BARGAIN-BASEMENT PARADISES.

THINK FOR A MOMENT, OR AS CLOSE TO IT AS YOU CAN. LET'S SAY TEMPTO'S CALLING THE SHOTS HERE, AND HE DOESN'T WANT TO BE FOUND. HE'S GOING TO WANT A WILD PLACE--

YUHYOU MEAN...

THAT'S RIGHT, PUDGIE--THE NEGATION OF ALL THIS PAT NONSENSE.

BUHBUT CAIN...

QUIET! I WANT THREE SHARES OF *NIHILISM* HERE!

--WHERE THINGS AREN'T OBVIOUS, AND THERE AREN'T A LOT OF RULES.

NUHNOW WHAT?

HOW SHOULD I KNOW? WHY IS IT *I* HAVE TO FIGURE OUT EVERYTHING?

BUHBUH BUH....

OH, STOP BLITHERING. WHATEVER LITTLE MENTAL ENERGY YOU HAVE HANDY OUGHT TO GO TOWARDS TRYING TO FIGURE OUT WHERE WE ARE.

WE'RE NUHNOWHERE. THERE'S NOTHING HERE, REMEMBER? AT LEAST NOT NUHNOW, IT CUHCOULD CHANGE.

NO DOUBT FOR THE WORSE.

HOW ABOUT YOU, GREGORY? HAVE ANY IDEA WHERE WE GO FROM HERE?

AWK.

HUMPH. THAT FIGURES. WELL, WHEREVER THIS IS, IT'S *HOT*.

LUHLOOK, CAIN. WHUWHAT ARE THOSE?

HMM. LOOKS LIKE A GROVE OF TREES. MAYBE IT'S AN OASIS OF SOME SORT.

CUHCAIN--THOSE AREN'T TREES. THEY'RE FUHFUH*FEET*.

GRRRRR.

I CAN *SEE* THAT, MUTTONFACE. ODD, TO BE SURE, BUT WE CAN STILL SIT UNDER THEM FOR A FEW MINUTES WHILE WE FIGURE OUT WHAT TO DO NEXT.

45

BLAM! BLAM!

G'DAY, MATES. SORRY TO BREAK UP YER LITTLE WRESTLIN' MATCH, BUT BIZNISS IS BIZNISS, AN' I GOT A SCHEDULE TA KEEP.

JUPITER'S CORNS, WHAT'S GOING ON HERE? WHO ARE YOU, AND WHAT ARE THESE MONSTROSITIES?

THEY CALL ME UNIPOD ED, AN' THESE HERE, A' COURSE, ARE UNIPODS. NOT FROM TERRA INCOGNITA, ARE YA, MATE? 'COURSE, SEEIN' AS YOU WAS THINKIN' TA CATCH SOME WINKS UNDER A UNIPOD FOOT, THAT GOES WITHOUT SAYIN'.

TERRA INCOGNITA. THAT'S THE PLACE ON THE OLD MAPS.

THAT'S RIGHT, MATE. "HERE BE MONSTERS," AN' ALL.

THAT'S JUST IGNORANCE, A' COURSE. AIN'T NO MORE MONSTERS HERE THAN ANYWHERE ELSE. NOT THAT A UNIPOD AIN'T AN UGLY BUGGER. GOOD EATIN', THOUGH, IF IT DON'T EAT YOU FIRST.

BLESS MY BOOTS--YOU PLAN TO EAT THOSE THINGS?

NOT THE WHOLE THING, MATE-- JIST THE FEET. THAT'S TH' TENDER PART. AN' NOT THIS LOT. THESE ARE FOR A SHIP'S CAPTAIN, DOWN ON THE BEACH.

ALL RIGHT, MEN. TROW DOSE TINGS IN DA DINGHY, AN' LET'S BE GONE.

46

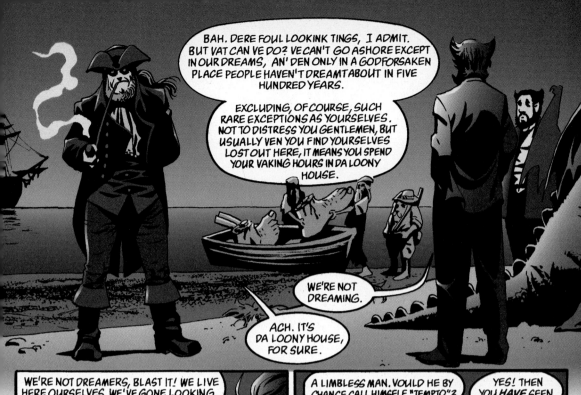

BAH. DERE FOUL LOOKINK TINGS, I ADMIT. BUT VAT CAN VE DO? VE CAN'T GO ASHORE EXCEPT IN OUR DREAMS, AN' DEN ONLY IN A GODFORSAKEN PLACE PEOPLE HAVEN'T DREAMT ABOUT IN FIVE HUNDRED YEARS.

EXCLUDING, OF COURSE, SUCH RARE EXCEPTIONS AS YOURSELVES. NOT TO DISTRESS YOU GENTLEMEN, BUT USUALLY VEN YOU FIND YOURSELVES LOST OUT HERE, IT MEANS YOU SPEND YOUR VAKING HOURS IN DA LOONY HOUSE.

WE'RE NOT DREAMING.

ACH. IT'S DA LOONY HOUSE, FOR SURE.

WE'RE NOT DREAMERS, BLAST IT! WE LIVE HERE OURSELVES. WE'VE GONE LOOKING FOR SOMETHING, AND WE'VE GOTTEN A BIT OFF TRACK.

A BABY GOLDEN GARGOYLE, TO BE PRECISE. IT'S IN THE COMPANY OF A LIMBLESS MAN. HAVE YOU SEEN IT?

A LIMBLESS MAN. VOULD HE BY CHANCE CALL HIMSELF "TEMPTO"?

YES! THEN YOU *HAVE* SEEN THEM?

VELL, NOW DAT YOU MENTION IT, I HAF SEEN VAT YOU'RE LOOKINK FOR. CHUST A SHORT TIME AGO DEY SHIPPED OUT VEST FROM HERE, A ROUTE I KNOW VELL.

IF YOU VANT, I CAN TAKE YOU DAT VAY. ALL I'D ASK IN RETURN IS A COUPLE GAMES OF CHESS.

CUHCAIN...DUHDO YOU THINK HE'S RUHREALLY SEEN GUHGOLDIE?

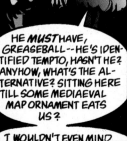

HE *MUST* HAVE, GREASEBALL--HE'S IDENTIFIED TEMPTO, HASN'T HE? ANYHOW, WHAT'S THE ALTERNATIVE? SITTING HERE TILL SOME MEDIAEVAL MAP ORNAMENT EATS US?

I WOULDN'T EVEN MIND A FEW ROUNDS OF CHESS. GOODNESS KNOWS, I CAN'T PLAY IT WITH *YOU*.

ALL RIGHT, CAPTAIN-- YOU'VE GOT YOURSELF A DEAL. I WARN YOU, THOUGH-- I'M NOT EXACTLY INEXPERIENCED IN THE NOBLE ART OF CRUSHING CHESS OPPONENTS.

NO QUARTER ASKED, NO QUARTER GIVEN. I VOULDN'T HAVE IT ANY UDDER WAY.

AND WHAT DID YOU SAY WAS THE NAME OF YOUR SHIP AGAIN?

DEY CALL IT DA DUTCHMAN, DA FLYINK DUTCHMAN.

CHECKMATE.

DRAT!

ACH, DON'T FEEL BAD. YOU'RE IMPROVING. YOU LASTED ALMOST FIVE MINUTES DIS TIME. C'MON, SET 'EM OP AGAIN.

I TOLD YOU, THIS WAS THE LAST TIME. I'M NOT PLAY-ING ANYMORE.

AW, COME ON. I'LL GIVE YOU DA AD-VANTAGE DIS TIME. I VON'T USE MY QUEEN.

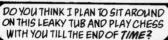

DO YOU THINK I PLAN TO SIT AROUND ON THIS LEAKY TUB AND PLAY CHESS WITH YOU TILL THE END OF *TIME*?

VY NOT? Y'KNOW, I LIKE YOUR SPIRIT. IF YOU KEEP IMPROVINK, IN A HUNDRET YEARS OR SO, VE'LL BE ABLE TO REALLY PLAY.

I CAN'T SPARE A HUNDRED YEARS, OR EVEN A HUNDRED MORE MINUTES. WHAT'S REALLY GOING ON HERE, CAPTAIN? I'M BEGINNING TO THINK YOU LIED TO US!

VELL, MAYBE I STRETCHED TINGS A LITTLE VEN I SAID I'D SEEN YOUR GARGOYLE.

I *HAVE* SEEN TEMPTO, THOUGH. ABOUT SEVENTY-FIVE YEARS AGO. HE VAS STOWING AVAY ON DA *LUSITANIA.*

I DON'T KNOW VAT YOU VANT WIT DAT GUY. HE ISN'T ANY GOOD.

HE ISN'T ANY GOOD? AND WHAT ARE *YOU*, YOU POLDER-BRAINED DUTCH ABORTION? YOU HAVE NO *INTENTION* OF TAKING US WHERE WE WANT TO GO, EVEN IF YOU KNOW WHERE IT IS.

VELL, I SUPPOSE YOU HAVE A POINT. BUT, PUT YOURSELF IN *MY* POSITION. HOW WOULD *YOU* LIKE TO BE CON-DEMNED TO SAIL CEASELESSLY TILL JUDGMENT DAY VITH NO COMPANY BUT A CREW OF IGNORANT EX-CRIMINALS? DEY CAN'T EVEN *READ*, LET ALONE PLAY CHESS, AN' ANYVAY, DEY HATE ME.

I HAVE NO *INTENTION* OF BEING IN YOUR POSITION! I WANT OFF, DO YOU HEAR? I DEMAND TO BE TAKEN ASHORE IMMEDIATELY.

SORRY, BUT SHORE IS OUT OFF DA QVESTION. DA BEST I CAN DO IS A DINGHY AN' ENOUGH WATER FOR TWO DAYS.

I MIGHT JUST TAKE YOU *UP* ON THAT, YOU GOD-FORSAKEN EN-CRUSTATION ON THE SOLE OF A WOODEN SHOE.

SIXTEEN MUHMUHMEN ♪ ON A DUHDUHDEAD MAN'S CHEST, YUHYUHYUHYO HO HUHHO AN' A BUH- ♪ BUHBUH... ♪

HUHHUHHELLO, CAIN.

SHUT UP, YOU AMBULANT CATASTROPHE. HAVEN'T YOU CAUSED *ENOUGH* TROUBLE?

HUH? WHU-WHAT DID I DO?

YOU CONVINCED ME TO LET THAT DEVIL OF A CAPTAIN TAKE US PRISONER ABOARD THIS FLOATING NIGHTMARE.

BUHBUHBUT CAIN ... WUHWE'RE NOT PRISONERS. HE'S TUHTAKING US TO FUHFIND GOLDIE.

AND MY LEFT BIG TOE IS THE KING OF SPAIN. BLAST IT, HE HASN'T THE SLIGHTEST INTENTION OF DOING *ANYTHING*, SAVE PERHAPS BEAT ME AT CHESS TILL THE SECOND COMING.

THIS SHIP'S CONDEMNED TO SAIL *FOREVER*, AND SO ARE *WE*, IF WE DON'T FIND A WAY TO GET OFF IT.

OH, CUHCAIN, IT'LL BUHBE ALL RIGHT.

I WAS WUHWORRIED TOO, BUT I'VE TUHTALKED TO THE CUHCAPTAIN, AND HE SUHSEEMS LIKE A VERY NUHNICE FELLOW. IN FACT, I WUHWAS JUST ON MY WUHWAY TO HIS CABIN.

HE TUHTOLD ME HE'D TUHTUHTEACH ME TO PUHPLAY CHESS.

IDIOT!

SLAP!

♪ TWO MILLION ♪
SIX THOUSAND THREE HUNDRED FIFTY
FOUR BOTTLES OF BEER ON THE WALL... ♪♪♪

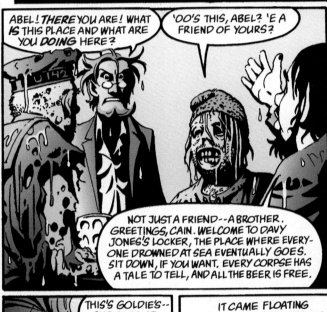

ABEL! *THERE* YOU ARE! WHAT *IS* THIS PLACE AND WHAT ARE YOU *DOING* HERE?

'OO'S THIS, ABEL? 'E A FRIEND OF YOURS?

NOT JUST A FRIEND--A BROTHER. GREETINGS, CAIN. WELCOME TO DAVY JONES'S LOCKER, THE PLACE WHERE EVERYONE DROWNED AT SEA EVENTUALLY GOES. SIT DOWN, IF YOU WANT. EVERY CORPSE HAS A TALE TO TELL, AND ALL THE BEER IS FREE.

IT LOOKS JOLLY, BUT IT'S TIME TO SAY GOODBYE AND COME ALONG. WE'RE *NOT* GOING TO FIND GOLDIE IN AN UNDERWATER TAVERN FULL OF DEAD PEOPLE.

DON'T BE SO SURE. LOOK.

THIS'S GOLDIE'S-- SHE TOOK IT FROM THE HOUSE.

WHAT? WHERE'D YOU *GET* THAT?

IT CAME FLOATING DOWN FROM OFF A BEACH NOT FAR FROM HERE. IT LOOKED TO *ME* AS IF SOMEONE HAD *THROWN* IT.

WELL, THAT'S ALL THE MORE REASON TO *LEAVE*.

SORRY, OLD MAN, BUT NO CAN DO. I'M STILL DEAD. YOU DROWNED ME. WE HAVE TO WAIT TILL I'M ALIVE AGAIN.

51

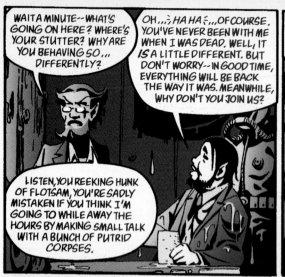

WAIT A MINUTE--WHAT'S GOING ON HERE? WHERE'S YOUR STUTTER? WHY ARE YOU BEHAVING SO... DIFFERENTLY?

OH...; HA HA;... OF COURSE. YOU'VE NEVER BEEN WITH ME WHEN I WAS DEAD. WELL, IT *IS* A LITTLE DIFFERENT. BUT DON'T WORRY--IN GOOD TIME, EVERYTHING WILL BE BACK THE WAY IT WAS. MEANWHILE, WHY DON'T YOU JOIN US?

LISTEN, YOU REEKING HUNK OF FLOTSAM, YOU'RE SADLY MISTAKEN IF YOU THINK I'M GOING TO WHILE AWAY THE HOURS BY MAKING SMALL TALK WITH A BUNCH OF PUTRID CORPSES.

'ERE, YOU, I'VE 'AD ABOUT ENOUGH OF THIS! THAT THERE'S ABEL, KEEPER OF SECRETS, AN' BROTHER OR NOT, LIVE MAN, IF YOU DON'T RESPECT HIM YOU'LL ANSWER TO ME.

UND ME!

NOW, NOW. CAIN DOESN'T WANT ANY TROUBLE.

LOOK, MAYBE YOU AND GREGORY OUGHT TO GO WAIT OVER THERE, OUT OF THE WAY. I'VE GOT A LOT OF FRIENDS HERE, AND THEY DON'T UNDERSTAND HOW IT IS WITH US.

HMPH.

CAROLINA

THREE MILLION SIX THOUSAND FIVE HUNDRED SEVENTY TWO BOTTLES OF BEER ON THE WALL...

I HAD ANOTHER DREAM.

OH YEAH?

Y'KNOW, I'M GOOD AT INTERPRETING DREAMS. DID YOU SEE WATER, OR TRAINS GOING INTO TUNNELS?

NO. I SAW EDEN. AS IT WAS IN THE BEGINNING.

IT WAS LIKE IT WAS REAL, NOT A MEMORY. I'M NOT SURE I HAVE MEMORIES OF EDEN. I'M NOT SURE I WAS EVER ACTUALLY THERE.

IT WAS BEAUTIFUL, THOUGH. AND HE WAS IN IT AGAIN.

WHO?

THE SNAKE.

HE WAS DIFFERENT THIS TIME. HE HAD HIS ARMS AND LEGS AGAIN, LIKE HE DID IN THE GARDEN.

HE WAS BEAUTIFUL. I'D FORGOTTEN HOW BEAUTIFUL HE WAS. I WANTED TO JOIN HIM.

DO YOU WANT TO STILL?

NO. IT'S SOME KIND OF TRICK, I KNOW -- IT ALWAYS IS WITH HIM.

BUT WHY IS THIS COMING UP NOW, MATTHEW? WHAT'S GOING ON?

CUHCUHCUH-CAIN! CUHCUHCUH-CAIN!

≥HUNF!≤ WHA...

ABEL! YOU'RE BACK, AND YOU'RE YOUR OLD SELF.

FUHFUHFUHFOR A WUHWUHWHILE. WUHWANT SOME CUHCOFFEE?

WHAT HAPPENED? THE LAST THING I REMEMBER IS FOUR MILLION BOTTLES OF BEER.

YOU FELL ASUHSLEEP, CAIN. I HUHHAD TO LUH-LEAVE WHEN I SUHSTOPPED BUH-BEING DEAD, SO GUGUHGREGORY TUHTOOK US HERE.

AND WHERE IS HERE, MAY I ASK?

I DUHDUH-DON'T KNOW.

BUHBUHBUT IT DOESN'T LOOK LUHLIKE ANYONE'S BUH*BEEN* HERE FOR AWUHWHILE.

YOU MEAN YOU DON'T EVEN KNOW WHERE THIS DESOLATE BONEYARD YOU'VE BROUGHT US TO *IS?*

NUHNUHNUHNO. BUHBUHBUT IT'S WHERE GUHGOLDIE'S PICTURE GUHGOT THROWN FUHFROM.

AND WHO TOLD YOU *THAT?* SOME BLOATED, FISH-EATEN CADAVER?

BUHBUH-BUHBUH,,,,

SHUT UP, ABEL! THIS TIME YOU *MUST'VE* SET SOME SORT OF RECORD FOR WITLESS IDIOCY! AND OF COURSE, IT'S LEFT TO *ME* TO TRY TO FIGURE OUT WHAT TO DO!

WE'LL NEED A SHELTER, FIRST OF ALL. WE COULD BE HERE FOR *CENTURIES!*

DAMMIT, STOP THAT GIBBERING! I'M TRYING TO THI,,,,

BUHBUH-BUHBUH ,,,

WHAT'S *THIS?* GOLDIE'S BASKET! SO SHE *IS* HERE! WHY DIDN'T YOU *TELL* ME YOU'D FOUND IT?

IT WUHWAS GUH-GUHGREGORY. WE WERE JUHJUST WUHWAITING FOR YOU TO WUHWAKE UP.

WELL, TOAST ME, BUTTER ME AND SERVE ME WITH JAM! AND HE'S ALREADY FOUND HER SCENT AGAIN, TOO! DON'T JUST STAND THERE -- LET'S *GO!*

THUTHUTHUTHESE RUHRUINS GO A LUHLONG *WAY!*

INDEED.

YOU KNOW, IT'S STRANGE, BUT I HAVE A FUNNY FEELING ABOUT THIS PLACE.

THE STYLE OF THESE CARVINGS...THOSE MOUNTAINS. I *KNOW* THEM. I'VE *BEEN* HERE BEFORE.

BUT HOW? WHEN? IT DOESN'T SEEM POSSIBLE. YET, THE FEELING GROWS MORE POWERFUL THE FARTHER WE GO.

CUHCUH-CUHCUH-CUH...

LUHLUH-LUH*LOOK!*

BLESS MY BEARD! I CAN'T BELIEVE IT, BUT THERE IT IS!

The Dreaming

BUT IT ALL DID HAPPEN. I WAS THE FIRST KING. I BUILT THIS PLACE, AND RULED IT FOR TWO HUNDRED YEARS. THE FIRST CITY, THE FIRST CIVILIZATION.

WHAT WAS HE LIKE?

WHO?

YOUR SUH-SON.

OH, I DON'T KNOW. FOR SOME REASON, I PICTURE HIM WITH A MOUSTACHE. HE RULED A HUNDRED AND FIFTY YEARS. A LONG TIME, EVEN THEN.

THUH-THEN WHAT HAPPENED?

THE WORLD, AS IT TENDS TO DO, GOT WORSE. THERE WERE WARS, REVOLTS. THEY TRIED TO BUILD A TOWER TO HEAVEN, AND *THAT* ENDED BADLY. AND THEN THERE WAS THE FLOOD.

IT ALL LED TO NOTHING. JUST A PHENOMENAL WASTE.

DO YOU THUH THINK HE MUH MIGHT STILL BE AROUND SOMEWHERE?

WHO?

ENOCH.

HOW SHOULD I KNOW? TILL A SHORT TIME AGO, I DIDN'T REMEMBER ANY OF THIS HAD EVEN *OCCURRED.*

IF WE DUH *DID* FIND HIM, MAYBE HE'D CALL ME "UNCLE ABEL." I'D RUH REALLY LIKE THAT.

IT'S JUHJUST BEEN THE TWO OF US FOR SO LONG...

ABEL, WHAT *ARE* YOU BLATHERING ABOUT?

WHAT WE ARE NOW HAS *NOTHING* TO DO WITH WHAT WE WERE THEN. THE FACT THAT I ONCE HAD A SON IS OF NO MORE RELEVANCE THAN THE FACT THAT YOU ONCE HERDED *SHEEP!*

"UNCLE ABEL!"

ABEL, IF YOU DON'T STOP GIBBERING ABOUT YOUR SUPPOSED NEPHEW, I'M GOING TO...

GRK.

I SWEAR--IF THE REST OF OUR FAMILY BEARS ANY RESEMBLANCE TO *YOU,* THEN RELATIVES ARE THE *LAST* THING WE NEED TO FIND.

WELL, GOLDIE, HERE WE ARE.

THE GOLDIE FACTOR
PART THREE

TERRY LaBAN, writer
PETER SNEJBJERG, artist
DANIEL VOZZO, colorist & seps
TODD KLEIN, letterer
ALISA KWITNEY, editor
NEIL GAIMAN, consultant

The Dreaming created by
NEIL GAIMAN

IMPRESSIVE, ISN'T IT?

THEY'VE KEPT VISITORS OUT SINCE THE BEGINNING OF TIME. BUT NOT *US.*

I'M WITH HER.

LOOK AT IT, GOLDIE. NO LIVING CREATURE HAS SEEN THIS PLACE SINCE WE WERE EXPELLED, COUNTLESS MILLENNIA AGO.

SEE? YOU'RE A CELEBRITY.

YOU COULD FIND EVERY PLANT AND ANIMAL IN THE WORLD HERE ONCE. THE STREAMS WERE CLEAR AND SWEET, AND THE TREES WERE HEAVY WITH FRUIT.

OOF!

MAYBE YOU'D DO BETTER WITHOUT LEGS *YOURSELF*, YOU OAF. NEXT TIME YOU FALL, I'LL LEAVE YOU THERE.

SUHSUH-SUHSORRY, CUHCUH...

SAVE YOUR WIND. COME ON! HE'S GONE OVER THAT RIDGE.

LOOK! HE'S STOPPED. I DON'T SEE GOLDIE, THOUGH.

WUHWHUHWHUH-WHAT'S THAT THING?

IT LOOKS LIKE SOME KIND OF *NEST*. MADE OF... THOSE AREN'T BRANCHES, ARE THEY?

THUHTHEY'RE BUH*BONES*! GUH-GOLDEN BONES!

GREGORY, WHAT *IS* THIS? IS GOLDIE *HIDING* IN THERE?

CUHCUHCAIN! LUHLOOK!

GAD! IT'S A SKELETON!

IT'S GUHGOLD TOO!

GREGORY, STOP THAT!

AWROOOO!

WHY'S HE MAKING THAT RACKET?

I DUHDON'T KNOW. MUH-MAYBE 'CUZ OF ALL THE DEAD GARGOYLES.

BLAST IT, I WISH SOMEONE WOULD TELL ME WHAT'S GOING ON! IS THIS GOLDIE? DID SHE SUDDENLY GET BIG AND DIE? IF NOT, WHY DID GREGORY TAKE US HERE?

MUHMAYBE IT SUHSMELLED LIKE GOLDIE. MAYBE IT'S GOLDIE'S HOME.

BUT CLEARLY, GOLDIE ISN'T HERE NOW! IF THIS IS AS FAR AS GREGORY CAN TAKE US, THEN I'D SAY WE'RE IN A PECK OF TR...

AWK!

AWK!

LOOK--THERE'S SOMETHING DOWN THERE! IT LOOKS ALMOST LIKE A FARM OF SOME SORT.

COME ON, JIGGLES--TIME TO LOSE A FEW MORE POUNDS.

≳PUFF!≲ ≳PANT!≲ I JUST HOPE THIS TIME HE TAKES US TO GOLDIE!

YOU SEE, GOLDIE? THERE'S NOTHING TO FEAR, AND EVERYTHING TO LOOK FORWARD TO.

IN JUST A LITTLE WHILE, THE FALL WILL NEVER HAVE HAPPENED. EDEN WILL AGAIN BLOOM AND BE FRUITFUL. HATRED AND VIOLENCE WILL CEASE. AND YOU'LL HAVE DONE IT. WHAT A GIFT YOU'RE GIVING TO THE WORLD.

NOW--PUT YOUR FOOT ON THE STONE AT THE CENTER OF MY TURBAN.

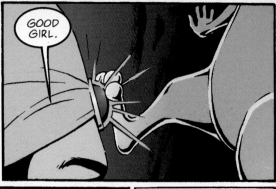

GOOD GIRL.

DO YOU FEEL THAT? CALM. BE CALM NOW, AND LISTEN.

"NOW THE SERPENT WAS THE SHREWDEST OF ALL THE WILD BEASTS THAT THE LORD HAD MADE.

"HE SAID TO THE WOMAN, 'DID GOD REALLY SAY: YOU SHALL NOT EAT OF ANY TREE OF THE GARDEN'?

"THE WOMAN REPLIED TO THE SERPENT: 'WE MAY EAT OF THE FRUIT OF THE OTHER TREES OF THE GARDEN. IT IS ONLY THE FRUIT OF THE TREE IN THE MIDDLE OF THE GARDEN THAT GOD SAID: YOU SHALL NOT EAT OF IT OR TOUCH IT, LEST YOU DIE.'

"AND THE SERPENT SAID TO THE WOMAN: 'YOU ARE RIGHT.

"'TO EAT OF THE TREE WOULD BE CERTAIN DEATH.

"'REFRAIN FROM TASTING ITS FRUIT, AND DWELL PEACEFULLY IN EDEN UNTIL THE END OF TIME!'

"AND SHE DID REFRAIN, AND SO, DWELT THERE FOREVER."

THE END.

MY ARMS... MY LEGS... IT'S WORKING!

I CAN WALK, I CAN STAND, I CAN GRAB AND HOLD!

HA HA HA! IT'S WORKING!

LOOK-- REALITY'S REVERSING ITSELF. EVERYTHING FORMED SINCE THE FALL IS WHIRLING BACKWARDS INTO THE SOURCE.

IT NEVER HAPPENED.

"AND IT NEVER WILL."

WHAT'S GOING ON? WHERE AM I?

THE TREES AND FLOWERS... ALL THIS FRUIT... AM I DREAMING OF THE GARDEN AGAIN?

NO, EVE. THIS TIME, YOU'RE REALLY HERE.

YOU!

YES. WE'RE BACK IN EDEN NOW. WE CAN START OVER, FREE FROM SIN. LIVE FOREVER IN PARADISE, AND NEVER FALL.

I DON'T BELIEVE IT! IT'S A TRICK. I'LL WAKE UP IN MY CAVE IN AN HOUR AND MAKE SOME TEA TO CALM MY MIND.

YOU WON'T NEED YOUR CAVE ANYMORE, OR YOUR TEA. THERE'S NOTHING TO WORRY ABOUT. EVERYTHING'S PERFECT, PEACEFUL AND INNOCENT.

NOW LISTEN, YOU...

EVE!

THERE YOU ARE. LOOK AT THIS!

ISN'T IT JUST THE NEATEST CREATURE? I THINK I'M GOING TO CALL IT A "TURTLE."

WONDERFUL, ADAM. YOU HAVE SUCH A FACILITY FOR NAMING THINGS. DOESN'T HE, EVE?

WHY DON'T YOU KIDS RUN ALONG NOW? I NOTICED SOME REALLY FASCINATING ANIMALS WANDERING DOWN BY THE RIVER, AND I'M SO ANXIOUS TO SEE WHAT YOU'LL END UP CALLING THEM.

LET GO OF ME! YOU THINK I'M GOING TO SPEND THE REST OF ETERNITY TAGGING ALONG AFTER THIS GUY WHILE HE THINKS OF A NAME FOR EVERY ORGANISM IN THE *UNIVERSE?*

CAN YOU THINK OF A *BETTER* WAY TO SPEND IT? EVE, LOOK--

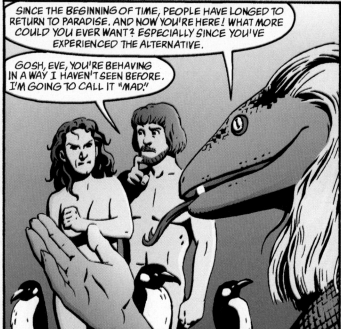

SINCE THE BEGINNING OF TIME, PEOPLE HAVE LONGED TO RETURN TO PARADISE. AND NOW YOU'RE HERE! WHAT MORE COULD YOU EVER WANT? ESPECIALLY SINCE YOU'VE EXPERIENCED THE ALTERNATIVE.

GOSH, EVE, YOU'RE BEHAVING IN A WAY I HAVEN'T SEEN BEFORE. I'M GOING TO CALL IT "MAD."

I DON'T KNOW WHAT I WANT, BUT IT ISN'T THIS. THERE'S PLENTY IN THE EBB AND FLOW OF HUMAN HISTORY I HAVEN'T LIKED, BUT I CAN'T PRETEND IT NEVER HAPPENED. IT'S PART OF ME NOW, AND I WON'T LET YOU JUST WIPE IT ALL AWAY.

ADAM, STOP HER! SHE'S GOING TO EAT THE FORBIDDEN FRUIT!

EVE, WHAT ARE YOU DOING? YOU KNOW WE'RE NOT SUPPOSED TO DO THAT.

LET ME GO, ADAM!

THANK YOU, MR. SERPENT. THAT WAS CLOSE!

COME ON, EVE. LET'S GO DOWN TO THE RIVER. I WANT TO START FIGURING OUT WHAT TO CALL ALL THOSE THINGS THAT SWIM IN IT.

MY GOODNESS, LOOK AT THAT THING!

73

CUHCAIN... WHUWHERE *ARE* WE?

THE SAME PLACE WE WERE A FEW MINUTES AGO, I THINK.

LUHLUHLOOK! THUHTHERE'S GOLDIE!

AND EVE!

GUHGUHGUHGUH GOLDIE! WUHWE'VE BEEN LOOKING ALL *OVER* FOR YOU.

THE FEELING MAY NOT BE MUTUAL, GOLDIE, BUT *I'M* GLAD TO SEE YOU AS WELL. AND EVE -- THIS *IS* A SURPRISE.

FOR ME AS WELL.

WELL, HOW ABOUT THAT? YOU KNOW, I THINK THIS IS THE FIRST HAPPY REUNION I'VE EVER HAD.

Meep.

≩SOB≩....

≩SOB≩.... LOST. IT'S ALL LOST, AGAIN, FOREVER.

AWK!

WELL, WHAT DO YOU KNOW? IT'S THE GREAT TEMPTO HIMSELF.

GRRRRR

STAND BACK! I CAN SPIT VENOM THAT'LL BURN OFF YOUR SKIN, AND I'M DEADLY ACCURATE AT A HUNDRED FEET.

I DON'T BELIEVE YOU, SNAKE. YOUR TRICKS WON'T BAIL YOU OUT THIS TIME -- WE KNOW EVERYTHING ABOUT YOU.

IMBECILES! YOU KNOW *NOTHING*. NOT ONE STEP CLOSER, HEAR? WITH A MERE *GLANCE* I CAN REDUCE YOU ALL TO ASHES.

CAREFUL, CAIN.

HE'S LYING, OR HE'D HAVE DONE IT ALREADY. GET HIM, GREGORY!

HOLD IT! WHAT'S GOING ON? IS THERE ONE SNAKE OR *TEN*?

I...I CUHCAN'T SEE WHERE HE IS AT *ALL*.

AWK!

THIS IS WHERE THE GOLD GARGOYLES GUARD THE STORIES. ALL STORIES, BUT ESPECIALLY THE OLDEST ONES, THE ONES ALL THE OTHERS COME OUT OF.

GILGAMESH, THE LOTUS OF VISHNU, COYOTE AND THE OLD MAN, AND OF COURSE, THE GARDEN OF EDEN. IF YOU CHANGE THEM, YOU CHANGE EVERYTHING, DREAMING AND WAKING REALITY BOTH.

AND SO, GOLD GARGOYLES HAVE SAT HERE SINCE THE BEGINNING OF TIME, EACH ONE FOR A THOUSAND YEARS. YOU SEE, THEY WATCH OVER THE VERY FABRIC OF REALITY. IT'S AN AWESOME RESPONSIBILITY.

THAT ONE WAS THE LAST BEFORE YOU. IF ALL HAD GONE AS IT SHOULD, SHE'D HAVE HATCHED YOU AND TAUGHT YOU TO BE WHAT YOU ARE. ONLY THEN WOULD SHE HAVE DIED, AND YOU'D HAVE BUILT YOUR SECTION OF THE NEST WITH HER BONES.

BUT IN THE DREAMLORD'S ABSENCE, SOMETHING WENT WRONG. SHE DIED TOO SOON, AND YOUR EGG WAS STOLEN.

WUH-WHO STOLE IT, EVE? TUHTEMPTO?

MAYBE. HE'S ONE OF THE FEW WHO KNEW OF THIS PLACE, AND THERE WAS AN OLD STORY HE WANTED TO CHANGE DESPERATELY. BUT WE MAY NEVER KNOW FOR SURE.

BUT WE *DO* KNOW THAT GOLDIE'S BACK IN HER RIGHTFUL SPOT. YOU'RE VERY YOUNG YET, DEAR, BUT I'D VENTURE TO SAY NOW YOU KNOW BETTER THAN MOST OF YOUR PREDECESSORS WHAT IT IS YOU DEFEND, AND HOW IT IS YOU DEFEND IT.

WE NEED YOU, GOLDIE. ARE YOU READY?

Meep.

FOR GOODNESS' SAKE, ABEL, THIS REALLY *HAS* TO STOP.

I CUHCAN'T HUH*HELP* IT, CAIN. I MUHMISS GOLDIE.

I MISS HER TOO, ABEL, BUT LIFE GOES ON. CAN'T YOU CONSOLE YOURSELF EVEN A BIT WITH THE NOTION THAT THINGS HAVE BEEN SET RIGHT ONCE AGAIN?

NUHNO. NUHNOT REALLY.

I NEVER THOUGHT THE DAY *WOULD* COME WHEN I'D ACTUALLY WANT TO CHEER YOU UP, BUT I NEVER THOUGHT I'D BE DOING A *LOT* OF THINGS I'VE BEEN DOING OF LATE, SO I DON'T SUPPOSE I SHOULD BE SURPRISED.

I, UM... HAVE A PRESENT FOR YOU.

A PUH-PRESENT?

THAT'S RIGHT. HERE.

THIS ISN'T SUHSOME KIND OF TUHTRICK?

AFTER BERATING YOU ENDLESSLY ABOUT YOUR MOOD, WHAT POSSIBLE PLEASURE COULD I DERIVE FROM TRICKING YOU? AND EVEN IF I DID, IT COULDN'T MAKE YOU ANY MORE MISERABLE THAN YOU ALREADY *ARE*, COULD IT?

I GUH-GUESS NOT.

HOW BUHBEAUTIFUL. GOLD AND SILVER APPLES.

NOT APPLES. FRUIT FROM THE TREES OF KNOWLEDGE AND LIFE.

I PUT THEM IN MY POCKET BACK IN EDEN WHEN NO ONE WAS LOOKING. I WAS GOING TO KEEP THEM FOR MYSELF, BUT... I THOUGHT YOU MIGHT LIKE THEM.

THUHTHANK YOU, CAIN.

THAT'S IT? YOU DON'T SOUND VERY HAPPY.

NUHNO, I LIKE THEM. THEY'RE VERY NUH-NICE.

VERY *NICE*?

I'VE JUST GIVEN YOU TWO OF THE MOST VALUABLE ITEMS IN THE UNIVERSE, AND ALL YOU CAN SAY IS "VERY NICE"?

BLAST IT, YOU OOZING CLOT OF SELF-PITY, I HAVE HALF A MIND TO KILL YOU JUST TO PUT YOU OUT OF YOUR MISERY!

IS *THAT* WHAT YOU WANT?

MUHMAYBE.

WHAT DID YOU SAY?

MUHMAYBE YOU *SHOULD.* IT'S AWFUL, BUT...BUH-BEING HERE WITHOUT GUHGOLDIE IS WORSE.

ABSOLUTELY NOT! THAT'S NOT HOW IT WORKS. I DO IT BECAUSE *I* WANT TO!

PUHPLEASE, CAIN. YOU SAID YOU WUH-WANTED ME TO BUHBE HAPPY.

STRANGE. I'M NOT DEAD LIKE I USUALLY AM. I'M SOMEWHERE.

IT'S FAMILIAR. LIKE I'VE BEEN HERE. ALMOST LIKE...

Awk!

NO. IT *COULDN'T* BE...

GOLDIE! IT *IS* YOU!

AWK! AWK!

HOW STRANGE-- I'VE NEVER SEEN HIM LOOK SO PEACEFUL AND *HAPPY.* I DON'T KNOW WHY, BUT FOR SOME REASON ...

...I'M ALMOST SCARED.

END.

The
Lost
Boy

HELL'S TEETH.

MY LADY? IS ALL WELL?

NO. SADDLE MY HORSE.

MISTRESS, **CONSIDER**— IT IS NOT YET FOUR OF THE CLOCK AND STILL DARK ...

IF **ANYONE** MUST RIDE FORTH ON ERRAND — TO THE MAGISTRATE, IS IT? —

THEN THE DUTY SHOULD FALL TO **ME** ...

NO.

DAMMIT, SIR—ARE YOU **DEAF?** JUST SADDLE MY HORSE.

MY LADY, FROM YOUR MANNER I FEAR YOU SENSE SOME VILLAINY AFOOT— PERHAPS SOME DANGER TO YOUR PERSON. MAY I NOT AT LEAST **ACCOMPANY** YOU, LEST THERE BE RUFFIANS ABROAD?

HA! THE RUFFIAN HAS NOT BEEN **BORN**—

— THAT CAN AFFRIGHT **JOHANNA CONSTANTINE.**

FORGIVE ME, BROWN. YOUR GALLANTRY DOES YOU CREDIT. PERHAPS AN ESCORT **WOULD** BE PRUDENT ...

WAKE SIMPSON AND YOUNG JOHN, TELL THEM THEY RIDE WITH US. **AND** THEY ARE TO SPEAK OF THIS TO **NO ONE.**

AND BROWN ...

THIS IS A **PERSONAL** MATTER. IT REQUIRES **DISCRETION.**

I QUITE UNDERSTAND, MY LADY. YOU MAY RELY ON ME.

SORRY 'BOUT THER DELAY.

SEE, I WOZ GONNA 'AVE CHICKEN LARSE FRIDAY, ONLY I REALLY FANCIED A NICE BIT O' CHEESE INSTEAD.

YOU KNOW HOW IT IS.

nerrr...

BUT THER THING WITH CHEESE IS, ISS BUGGER ALL USE FOR FORETELLING ON ACCOUNT OF IT NOT BEIN' A DEAD ANIMAL.

BY THER TIME I FINALLY SEEN YOU, YOU WOZ MOVIN' ABOUT ALL OVER THE SHOP.

ISS TAKEN ME A WHILE TER FIND YOU.

STILL, NEVER MIND, EH? RIGHT AS RAIN AND RUBY SLIPPERS, THASS YOU NOW. OL' HETTIE'LL TAKE CARE OF YOU, YOU'LL SEE.

NOW I'M GONNER TAKE YOU TO A NICE DOCTOR FRIEND OF MINE. SHE'S A REAL LADY, SO MIND YER P'S AND Q'S.

ergh.

PITY YOU PONGS SO MUCH...

urrrr.

COLIN...

" 'COS IF I THINKS YOU PONGS, THEN YOU REALLY MUS' DO."

'OW THE FUCK DID WE GET DOWN 'ERE?

BLOOMSBURY, FORTY MINUTES LATER...

Briiing!

HELLO?

EVENIN', PERFESSER... I GOTTA **SURPRISE** FER YOU.

MAD **HETTIE**? DO YOU KNOW WHAT **TIME** IT IS?

'COURSE I DO. I AIN' GONE SOFT YET...

I BRUNG YOU A **PATIENT**, PERFESSER.

HETTIE, I'M **NOT** THAT SORT OF A DOCTOR.

AND THIS MAN **OBVIOUSLY** BELONGS IN A CASUALTY DEPARTMENT.

unnnh...

OR A DRUG CLINIC.

NAH. 'E'S A BIT BANGED UP, BUT 'E'S NOT A JUNKIE OR NUFFING.

'E MIGHT BE A BIT BE-FUSED AN' BE-MUDDLED, BUT **THASS** NOT WHY I BRUNG 'IM TO YER.

I BRUNG 'IM TO YOU 'COS 'E'S UNDER AN **ENCHANT-MENT.**

PROFESSOR—IS THIS YEAR **REALLY** 1996?

WHY, OF COURSE...

WHAT ELSE SHOULD IT BE?

I SAW A NEWSPAPER... A FEW DAYS AGO, AND I'VE SEEN... SO **MUCH** SINCE THEN, BUT...

BUT **I** KNOW IT'S **1956**... OH, HOW **CAN** THIS BE REAL? EITHER THE WORLD'S GONE MAD, OR **I** HAVE.

HAVE I, PROFESSOR?

WE DON'T REALLY **USE** TERMS LIKE THAT, MISTER SALMON. BUT...

NO, I DON'T THINK SO. NOT IN THE WAY THAT YOU MEAN.

RIGHT NOW I'M NOT SURE **WHAT** YOU ARE.

BUT I BELIEVE **YOU** BELIEVE THAT WHAT YOU'RE SAYING IS THE TRUTH.

AND SINCE YOU'VE PIQUED MY CURIOSITY, I **AM** GOING TO HELP YOU GET TO THE BOTTOM OF THIS.

NOW, WHY DON'T YOU PUT SOME **FOOD** INSIDE YOU, THEN GET YOURSELF CLEANED UP.

THEN WE'LL TALK AGAIN, ALL RIGHT?

YES, ALL RIGHT...

THE BATHROOM'S JUST DOWN THE HALL, AND I'VE LAID OUT A CHANGE OF CLOTHES FOR YOU.

I **THINK** THEY'LL FIT— THEY WERE MY BROTHER'S. I'LL SEE YOU DOWNSTAIRS.

THAT AFTERNOON.

NOW, YOU'RE **SURE** YOU FEEL UP TO TALKING ABOUT THIS?

JUST MAKE YOURSELF COMFORTABLE. I'VE CANCELLED MY STUDENTS TODAY, SO WE WON'T BE DISTURBED.

NOW, I WANT YOU TO RELAX, AND JUST TELL ME IN YOUR OWN WORDS...

YES,... I THINK SO. YOU CAN'T IMAGINE HOW GOOD IT FEELS TO FIND SOMEONE WHO **WILL** LISTEN.

AND I THINK,... IT'LL HELP, TO TELL SOMEONE.

BEFORE THINGS BEGAN TO SEEM.... **STRANGE** TO YOU, WHAT WAS THE LAST NORMAL THING YOU CAN REMEMBER? THE LAST ORDINARY, **NORMAL** THING?

LEWES...

"I'D BEEN TO SEE MY FIANCÉE, JOCELYN, FOR DINNER. SHE LIVED IN LEWES, DOWN NEAR BRIGHTON... I DON'T USUALLY SEE HER DURING THE WEEK, BUT WE HAD A LOT OF WEDDING ARRANGEMENTS TO DISCUSS..."

I **SAID** 'NO', BRIAN. NOW **STOP** IT.

WE AGREED TO **WAIT**. UNTIL THE WEDDING, REMEMBER?

I KNOW... IT'S JUST THAT, WELL... I **AM** HUMAN, JOSS.

IS **THAT** WHAT YOU CALL IT? NOW, WE'RE **SUPPOSED** TO BE CHOOSING OUR CURTAINS...

OH, GOD— DO WE **HAVE** TO?

"YOU SAID 'DURING THE WEEK'— CAN YOU RECALL THE DATE?"

"YES. IT WAS A THURSDAY. AND IT WAS MIDSUMMER'S EVE—

I REMEMBER BECAUSE JOSS'S FATHER MADE A RATHER LAME JOKE ABOUT BOTTOM DURING DINNER...

IT WAS JUNE 21ST, 1956."

YOU MIGHT SHOW A **BIT** OF INTEREST, CONSIDERING YOU'RE AN ARCHITECT. THIS **IS** GOING TO BE YOUR HOUSE, TOO, YOU KNOW.

YES, YOU'RE RIGHT. I'M SORRY.

I DON'T KNOW WHAT'S THE MATTER WITH YOU LATELY.

THE ONLY TIME I'VE SEEN YOU SHOW ANY ENTHUSIASM FOR ANYTHING — **APART** FROM THAT — WAS WHEN THAT R.A.F. CHAP AT TOM'S PARTY WAS GOING ON ABOUT **FLYING SAUCERS...**

WELL, YOU HAVE TO ADMIT IT **IS** JOLLY INTERESTING STUFF, DARLING.

IT'S **SILLY**, THAT'S WHAT IT IS. AND IT'S JUST TYPICAL OF YOU, BEING INTERESTED IN THAT AND IGNORING THE **IMPORTANT** THINGS.

HAVE YOU THOUGHT ANY MORE ABOUT THAT JOB OFFER?

NO. I THOUGHT YOU **UNDERSTOOD** — I DON'T WANT TO WORK FOR A BIG FIRM. I WANT TO DESIGN MY **OWN** BUILDINGS, NOT SOMEONE ELSE'S.

DADDY SAYS YOU JUST WANT TO TAKE FOOLISH RISKS TO MAKE UP FOR NOT SEEING ANY ACTION IN THE WAR...

THAT JUST **PROVES** WHAT AN ASS HE IS. I MIGHT HAVE BEEN STRAPPED TO A DESK BECAUSE OF MY **ASTHMA**...

BUT THE **WORK** I WAS DOING WAS **VITAL** TO THE WAR EFFORT.

DON'T CALL DADDY AN ASS. IT'S NOT **NICE.**

I'M SORRY, JOSS. LOOK, I KNOW I'M NOT THE **RICHEST** MAN IN THE WORLD, BUT...

WE'LL MANAGE. WE MIGHT HAVE TO MAKE **DO** FOR A WHILE, BUT...

I DON'T **WANT** TO "MAKE DO," BRIAN...

100

I WANT A **HOUSE**. A **PROPER** HOUSE. AND A BABY. AND I DON'T WANT TO WAIT **FOREVER** FOR THEM.

I THINK IT'S HIGH TIME YOU GREW **UP**, BRIAN.

IT'S GETTING LATE. I THINK I'D BETTER GO.

BE LIKE THAT THEN.

RUN AWAY, AS USUAL.

"SO I DROVE OFF, IN A BIT OF A HUFF. BACK TO MY FLAT IN LONDON. AND I'D GOT AS FAR AS THE ASHDOWN FOREST, WHEN ALL OF A SUDDEN…"

"…TUNED TO RADIO LUXEMBOURG. COMING RIGHT UP, THE ONE AND ONLY ELV—

"THE WIRELESS WENT DEAD. AND — MORE WORRYINGLY — SO DID THE CAR ENGINE.

"I MANAGED TO PULL IT OFF THE ROAD SAFELY, BUT IT STILL SHOOK ME UP QUITE A BIT.

"AND I WAS JUST SITTING THERE, LETTING MYSELF CALM DOWN AGAIN, WHEN… THREE GLOWING STREAKS **SHOT** ACROSS THE SKY.

"AND THEY SEEMED TO COME TO EARTH NOT FAR AWAY, UP IN THE WOODS.

"NOW ORDINARILY I'LL ADMIT I'M **NOT** THE BRAVEST OF SOULS. I JUST SAT THERE FOR AGES, TRYING TO DECIDE WHAT WAS THE **SENSIBLE** THING TO DO—

"—WHETHER I SHOULD STAY IN THE CAR, OR GET OUT AND START WALKING, TRY TO FIND A GARAGE.

"AND IN THE END, I DID NEITHER. I SUPPOSE IT WAS THE ARGUMENT WITH JOSS THAT DECIDED ME. I WASN'T GOING TO RUN AWAY FROM THIS."

RIGHT.

WE'LL SEE WHO'S BEING SILLY.

"SO I SET OFF, UP THE WOODED HILL. AND AS I WAS NEARING THE TOP, I HEARD VOICES.

FAUGH! WHAT HAVE THEY DONE TO THE AIR?

IT TASTES OF... METAL.

"**STRANGE** VOICES. ALMOST LIKE **SINGING**...

WELL, IT WAS **YOUR** IDEA TO COME HERE, RILLAINE.

AND A **FOOLISH** ONE IT WAS. SEE?

THERE IS NO BEACON LIT HERE.

THEY HONOUR THIS NIGHT NO LONGER, AND WE ARE **FORGOTTEN**.

"I CREPT UP, AS CLOSE AS I COULD, TRYING—PROBABLY NOT VERY SUCCESSFULLY—NOT TO MAKE ANY NOISE. AND THEN... I **SAW** THEM.

HA! I **NEVER** CARED FOR THIS PLANE ANYWAY.

BRAVO, MORTAL.

FOR THIS FAIR FLATTERY YOU SHALL HAVE A REWARD.

PAH! SO PREDICTABLE.

I TIRE OF THIS.

I WANT TO GO NOW.

I SEE YOU HAVE NOT YET MET YOUR OWN TRUE LOVE...

AND SO I GRANT YOU THIS BOON: WHEN NEXT YOU SLEEP, YOU SHALL DREAM OF HER...

MUCH GOOD WILL IT DO HIM.

OH, STOP TOYING WITH IT, RILLAINE.

PATIENCE, TRUANA THERE, 'TIS DONE.

FAREWELL THEN, MORTAL— OUR TRYST WILL NOT FIND FULFILLMENT, IT SEEMS.

SO I FEAR YOU MUST DESIRE ME HOPELESSLY, AND FOREVER.

HA, HA, HA...

COME ON.

THERE ARE FAIRER WORLDS WAITING TO AMUSE US...

LET US QUIT THIS MIDDEN.

"AND THEN THEY WERE GONE, AND THE WOODS WERE DARK AND DRAB WITHOUT THEM..."

"IT DIDN'T TAKE ME LONG TO WORK OUT THAT I WAS **TOTALLY** LOST. I HAD **NO** IDEA IN WHICH DIRECTION THE ROAD LAY, AND SINCE THERE'D BE NO ONE AROUND TO ASK UNTIL MORNING AT LEAST, I STARTED **WALKING. ANYTHING** SEEMED BETTER THAN JUST **STAYING** THERE.

"FRANKLY, I WAS AFRAID THOSE CREATURES MIGHT CHANGE THEIR MINDS AND COME BACK AGAIN.

"BUT I HADN'T GONE FAR BEFORE I DISCOVERED THAT I WAS **WRONG,** ABOUT THE CHANCES OF MY MEETING ANYONE."

NOW YOU DONE IT, BONNIE BOY...

YOU LOST YER **WAY,** AIN'CHER?

NOW YOU GOT TER GO BACK THER **PRITTY** ROUTE.

TO BE CONTINUED.

WOT YEAR IS IT? 00'S ON THER FRONE?

WHAT? OH, I SEE...

1956 AND QUEEN ELIZABETH, OF COURSE... LOOK, I'M PERFECTLY SANE, AND I DON'T MEAN YOU ANY HARM. I JUST WANT TO FIND THE ROAD AGAIN...

I RECKONS I CAN 'ELP YER. THERE'LL BE A PRICE, MIND...

THERE'S ALWAYS A PRICE, BONNY BOY.

LOOK, IF IT'S MONEY YOU WANT, I'M AFRAID I HAVEN'T MUCH ON ME...

NAH. MONEY DON'T GET YER NUFFINK WORF 'AVIN... TELL YER WOT, THO'— YOU CAN DO A LITTEL ERRAND FER ME. I'M GONNER GIVE YOU SOMEFINK TER LOOK AFTER, SEE?

YOU TAKE GOOD CARE OF IT, AN' I'LL COME AN' GET IT OFF YER LAYTER.

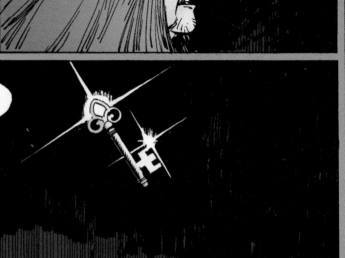

'ERE, CATCH.

THE LOST BOY

Part Two

Peter Hogan · Writer
Steve Parkhouse · Artist
Daniel Vozzo · Colors&Seps

Alisa Kwitney · Editor
Neil Gaiman · Consultant

The Dreaming created by Neil Gaiman

BUT...

JUS' YOU **DO** IT, ALL RIGHT?

AN' I'LL MAKE SURE YOU GETS 'OME SAFE AGAIN. ISSA **PROMISE**.

VERY WELL, IF YOU INSIST...

WE COULD SPIT ON IT, IF YER LIKE...

NO, I **DON'T** THINK THAT WILL BE **NECESSARY**.

JUST TELL ME WHERE THE **ROAD** IS, PLEASE.

SURTINLY. I GOT FINGS TER DO AN' ALL. ISS OVER THAT WAY, BONNIE BOY...

THANK YOU.

AN' DON' YOU WORRY ABOUT GETTIN' LOST—I'LL FIND YER.

"SO I WENT OFF, IN THE DIRECTION SHE'D INDICATED. WHEN I LOOKED BACK, SHE'D VANISHED..."

Heh heh heh...

WAS ONE OF THESE THE KEY?

NO...THOSE ARE MY HOUSE AND CAR KEYS. I PUT THE KEY SHE GAVE ME IN THE BREAST POCKET OF MY JACKET.

WELL, YOU DEFINITELY DIDN'T HAVE IT ON YOU WHEN HETTIE BROUGHT YOU HERE. UNLESS SHE TOOK IT...

BUT I DOUBT THAT...

SHE MAY BE A STRANGE OLD THING, BUT IN MY EXPERIENCE SHE'S ALWAYS SCRUPULOUSLY HONEST.

I EXPECT I JUST LOST IT. IT'S NOT IMPORTANT, IS IT?

WHO KNOWS? THOUGH I SHALL MAKE A POINT OF ASKING HETTIE ABOUT IT WHEN SHE TURNS UP.

YOU WERE SAYING— YOU LEFT THE OLD WOMAN...

"YES. THAT WAS THE LAST I SAW OF HER."

Heh heh heh.

ASHDOWN FOREST, JUNE 21st. 1827.

OVER THERE— DO YOU SEE HER?

'AN *THIS'LL* BE LADY LAH-DEE-BLEEDIN'-DAH.

YOU.

'COURSE.

WOZ YOU EXPECTIN' SOMEONE ELSE?

OR 'AS YOU GOT SO MANY ENEMIES NOW THAT YOU LOSES TRACK OF 'EM ALL?

JUST GIVE ME THE **KEY**, WOMAN.

HO, YES? **YORES**, IS IT? ONLY I SEEMS TO RECALL 'OW IT WOZ **YOU** WOT STOLE IT FROM **ME**.

YOU DON' EVEN KNOW WOT IT **OPENS**.

I KNOW FROM WHOM IT COMES —THAT SCOUNDREL **JEFFERSON**—

AND THAT IT LEADS TO **POWER**. I WILL **FIND** THE LOCK IN TIME...

BELIEVE ME. BROWN, **SEARCH** HER.

I WOODEN **TRY** IT, LUVVIE...

BESIDES, IT WON' DO YER NO GOOD. I AIN'T GOT IT.

I PROMISED I'D KEEP IT **SAFE**, AN' I 'AVE. I SENT IT SOMEWHERE YOU **CARN** GET AT IT.

I **COULD** HAVE YOU HANGED FOR A SPY.

HO, YES? AN' WOT ARE **YOU**, THEN?

I KNOWS **ALL** ABOUT YOU AN' THER **LITTEL** CORSICAN, JOHANNA CONSTANTINE.

AN' **BESIDES**...

YOU *DON'T* WANNER MESS WIV' ME, GIRLIE. I CAN DO FINGS YOU AIN'T EVEN *READ* ABOUT.

YOU *KNOWS* I CAN.

I MAKES A VERY PASSABLE *FRIEND*. I KNOWS WOT YOU *REALLY* WANTS, YER LADYSHIP. I MEAN, WOSS THER USE O' POWER WHEN YOU'RE SIX FEET UNDER, EH? *BUGGER ALL* IF Y'ARSK ME...

YOU WANTS A FEW MORE YEARS BEFORE YOU GOES OFF A-DANCIN' WIV THER *DARKLIN' GIRL* DON'CHER?

AN' I CAN *GIVE* YER THEM YEARS.

DAM' YOU, HENRIETTA...

HOW THE *UVVER 'AND*...

YOU WOULD... *ARRANGE* THIS FOR ME?

I WOULD... AN' IF YOU PROMISES TER STAY OUT O' THER WAY O' ME AN' MINE FROM NOW ON, I *WILL*.

NINETY NINE YEARS, AN' THASS MY FINAL OFFER.

VERY WELL — YOU HAVE MY WORD. OUR PATHS SHALL *NOT* CROSS AGAIN.

GOD BE WITH YOU, HENRIETTA. *HOME*, BROWN.

VERY GOOD, MY LADY.

AND WHAT HAPPENED WHEN YOU FOUND THE ROAD?

WELL, I DIDN'T -- NOT TILL NEXT MORNING, THAT IS.

I ... HEARD SOME STRANGE NOISES AND I PANICKED, AND STARTED RUNNING. THEN I MUST HAVE TRIPPED, AND KNOCKED MYSELF OUT ... I CAN REMEMBER DREAMING ...

"CAN YOU REMEMBER WHAT ABOUT?"

"NO, NOT REALLY. JUST THAT THERE WAS THIS MYSTERIOUS OLD HOUSE ..."

HELLO -- OH? IS THERE ANYBODY HOME?

YES?

AND WHO MIGHT YOU BE?

I'M, I'M ... WHERE AM I?

WHY, YOU'RE HERE.

OBVIOUSLY.

Hmmm. A FAIRY BOON, EH? YOU DON'T SEE TOO MANY OF *THOSE* THESE DAYS. YOU MUST BE A MOST *UNUSUAL* YOUNG MAN.

MY COMMISERATIONS.

NOW THEN, IS THIS 'TRUE LOVE' OR 'BURIED TREASURE'?

I'M SORRY?

YOUR BOON, OF COURSE. SLOW, AREN'T YOU?

UM, LOVE, I THINK...

AH, L'AMOUR! THE BIGGEST MYSTERY OF THEM ALL.

BUT OVERRATED, IF YOU ASK ME. AND YOUR NAME IS?

ER, SALMON. BRIAN SALMON.

INDEED? HOPING TO *SPAWN*, ARE WE? FUNNY, I ALWAYS THOUGHT SALMON COULD FIND THEIR WAY TO THE MATING GROUNDS *UNAIDED*...

BUT *YOU* OBVIOUSLY NEED ALL THE HELP YOU CAN *GET*. NOW, LET'S SEE... Salmon, Ella; Salmon, Rock... AH, *HERE* YOU ARE.

AND HOW *CONVENIENT*. YOUR YOUNG LADY IS DREAMING THIS VERY MOMENT. SO...

"MAY I HAVE THE *NEXT* CONTESTANT, PLEASE..."

FTOOM

Oh!

I...I WAS READING...

HOW VERY ENLIGHTENED OF YOU, MY DEAR.

A RIVETING TEXT, NO DOUBT, SINCE YOU ARE NOW FAST ASLEEP...

AND SO, ALLOW ME TO WELCOME YOU TO ANOTHER EDITION OF 'THIS IS YOUR LOVE'—THE POPULAR GAME FOR ALL AGES.

WHY, ALREADY YOU'VE WON A FABULOUS PRIZE!

TO WIT, THIS YOUNG MAN.

This is you[r]

DAD WAS RIGHT. I'VE BEEN STUDYING TOO HARD.

NOW, COME ALONG, COME ALONG. WE HAVEN'T GOT ALL NIGHT YOU KNOW.

YOUR DREAM CRUISE AWAITS...

RIGHT, IN YOU GET.

IS THIS THING SAFE?

DON'T BE RIDICULOUS.

TRUE LOVE MAY BE A LOT OF THINGS, BUT IT'S ALMOST NEVER "SAFE."

YOU CAN'T *RESIST* MEDDLING, CAN YOU?

DON'T YOU *EVER* LEARN, POOPBRAIN?

BUH BUH BUT *CAIN*— IT'S NOT EVEN A SUH SUH *SECRET.*

EVERYBODY KNUH *KNOWS* THE WUH WUH *WILD* WUH WUH *WOODS* ARE DANGEROUS...

YES, BUT THEY DON'T KNOW *WHY,* DO THEY?

THEY DON'T KNOW *HOW,* DO THEY?

DO THEY?

duh don't thu they?

NO. BECAUSE THOSE THINGS ARE *MYSTERIES*...

AREN'T THEY, DOLT?

Oh, duh duh dear...

STOP *BULLYING* HIM, YOU.

Hmmm? OH, YES...

I THINK YOU TWO HAD BETTER BE *GOING.* MY BROTHER AND I HAVE THINGS TO *DISCUSS.*

121

YES... YOU'VE STILL GOT A SLIGHT BRUISE THERE...

SO THEN WHAT HAPPENED?

WELL, AFTER I'D PULLED MYSELF TOGETHER, I CARRIED ON LOOKING FOR THE ROAD.

AND FOUND IT, EASILY ENOUGH...

"I'M ALMOST CERTAIN I EVEN FOUND THE STRETCH WHERE I'D LEFT THE CAR — BUT THERE WAS NO SIGN OF IT...

SO I STARTED WALKING.

I PLANNED TO REPORT THE CAR MISSING, THEN CATCH A TRAIN TO LONDON FROM FOREST ROW. THAT WAS THE NEAREST RAILWAY STATION, YOU SEE..."

"AT LEAST IT WAS A BEAUTIFUL SUMMER'S DAY. BUT I HADN'T GOT VERY FAR WHEN...

A LORRY HURTLED PAST ME AT A RATE OF KNOTS...

AND IT WAS THE BIGGEST, LONGEST LORRY I'D EVER SEEN."

"THEN I NOTICED THE CARS THAT WERE STARTING TO PASS ME. ALL OF THEM WERE STRANGE, LIKE SOMETHING OUT OF 'DAN DARE'...

LONG VEHICLE

"I KEPT WALKING. WHAT ELSE COULD I DO?

AND I SAW MORE THINGS THAT PUZZLED ME... STRANGE ADVERTISEMENTS ON THE SIDES OF VANS, A FUTURISTIC HOUSE..."

PROTECT YOUR SOFTWARE

QUANTUM SYSTEMS

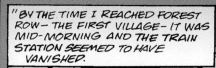

"BY THE TIME I REACHED FOREST ROW— THE FIRST VILLAGE— IT WAS MID-MORNING AND THE TRAIN STATION SEEMED TO HAVE VANISHED.

THOUGH I DON'T *NORMALLY* DRINK THAT EARLY IN THE DAY I REALLY FELT I NEEDED A GOOD STIFF WHISKY. SO, I WENT INTO A PUB..."

THANKS.

A SCOTCH, PLEASE. MAKE IT A LARGE ONE.

ARE YOU TAKING THE PISS?

I'M SORRY... I *HAVEN'T* ANYTHING SMALLER.

AND I REALLY DON'T THINK THERE'S ANY CALL FOR LANGUAGE.

WHAT'S UP, HARRY?

TROUBLE.

JOKER HERE ORDERS A DRINK, AND THEN GIVES ME *THIS*.

MY... A TEN-BOB NOTE! I HAVEN'T SEEN ONE OF THESE IN *YEARS*.

MUST BE A STUDENT PRANK.

BIT *OLD* FOR A STUDENT, AREN'T YOU, LOVE? YOU OUGHT TO *KNOW* BETTER.

WANT ME TO THROW HIM OUT, BETTY?

NAH. IT'S NOT WORTH THE *AGGRO*, HARRY. ANYWAY, THESE THINGS MUST BE WORTH A FEW QUID. WE MIGHT EVEN BE A FEW BOB *UP* ON THIS.

BUT WHAT ABOUT MY *CHANGE*?

CHARMING, I MUST SAY.

LOOK, DON'T *PUSH* IT, SUNSHINE. YOU'RE LUCKY I DON'T HAVE THE LAW ON YOU.

JUST FINISH YOUR DRINK AND SOD OFF.

COMPRENDAY?

"AND THEN I BORROWED THIS OLD CHAP'S NEWSPAPER...

AND I'D NEVER SEEN A PAPER *LIKE* IT."

"THERE *WASN'T* ANY NEWS — JUST SCANDAL ABOUT PEOPLE I'D NEVER HEARD OF. AND THERE WAS A *PINUP*, OF A GIRL WITH NO TOP ON..."

AND *THEN* I NOTICED THE DATE. I MUST HAVE STARED AT IT FOR A GOOD TEN MINUTES, I WAS SO RATTLED..."

Saturday, June 22, 1996   5

DI DOES DIRTY ON FRIENDS

"WHEN I COULD *MOVE* AGAIN, I FINISHED MY DRINK AND LEFT."

"IN THE VILLAGE, I PASSED SHOPS SELLING THINGS I DIDN'T EVEN **UNDERSTAND**...."

VILLAGE VIDEO

SAVER DEAL **2** for the price of **1**

SAVE on tapes!

2 for the price of ONE!

"I THOUGHT I MUST BE SUFFERING FROM CONCUSSION, FROM HITTING MY HEAD. I FORGOT ALL ABOUT REPORTING MY CAR MISSING. MY ONE THOUGHT WAS JUST TO GET **HOME**, TO LONDON...."

"I WAS SURE THAT IF I COULD ONLY GET TO MY OWN BED AND GET SOME SLEEP, MAYBE CALL THE DOCTOR IN THE MORNING, THEN I'D BE FINE.

SO I WALKED ON, TO EAST GRINSTEAD, AND CAUGHT A TRAIN TO VICTORIA.

NOBODY EVEN ASKED ME FOR A TICKET."

"THE STATION WAS STRANGE. THE TRAIN WAS STRANGE. THE THINGS I SAW THROUGH THE TRAIN WINDOW WERE STRANGE.

I FELT LIKE I WAS RUNNING A FEVER...."

"THEN I WAS SICK IN THE TOILET, AND FELT A LITTLE BETTER.

BUT EVEN THE TOILET PAPER WAS STRANGE...."

"AND LONDON WAS... MADNESS. EVERYTHING WAS FAMILIAR, BUT... WRONG.

AND I DIDN'T KNOW HOW TO PUT IT RIGHT AGAIN."

"I TRIED TO TAKE THE TUBE, BUT THE TICKET MACHINES WOULDN'T ACCEPT MY MONEY, SO I HAD TO WALK HOME, RIGHT ACROSS TOWN...

AND IT WAS THE CITY I KNEW, I WAS SURE OF IT— ALL THE LANDMARKS I KNEW WERE THERE. BUT IT WAS... AS IF IT HAD BEEN OVERLAID, WITH A NEW CITY.

A GRIMY, GAUDY GHASTLY ONE..."

"AND IT WASN'T JUST THE BUILDINGS AND THE CARS. THERE WAS LITTER EVERYWHERE. AND THE PEOPLE — THE WAY THEY DRESSED, AND LOOKED..."

"AND TALKED...

GIDDOUDA THE FUCKIN' ROAD, DICK'EAD.

WELL, THEY JUST WEREN'T LIKE PEOPLE — NOT LIKE ANY PEOPLE I'D EVER KNOWN..."

"AND WHEN I FINALLY REACHED MY HOME..."

"IT WASN'T **THERE.**"

"WHERE IT **OUGHT** TO HAVE BEEN THERE WAS A BRAND-NEW OFFICE BUILDING."

"THE COMMISSIONAIRE THERE LISTENED TO ME POLITELY, THEN TOLD ME HE'D CALL THE POLICE IF I DIDN'T STOP MAKING A SCENE AND LEAVE..."

"AFTER THAT I JUST WANDERED AIMLESSLY. MY MIND WAS REELING — I **KNEW** IT COULDN'T **REALLY** BE 1996 — I MEAN, HOW **COULD** IT BE?

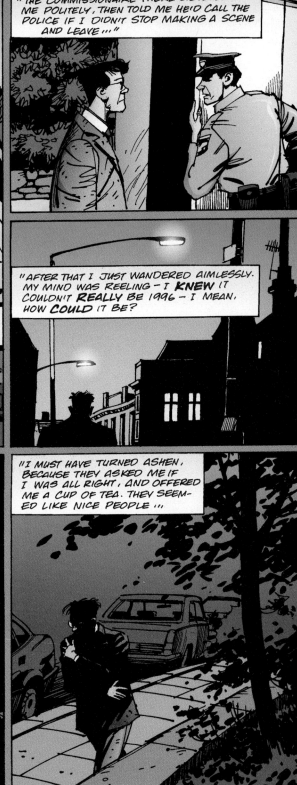

SO I THOUGHT I MUST BE **REALLY** ILL. I KNEW I NEEDED **HELP,** SO I WALKED ACROSS TOWN TO MY PARENTS' HOUSE. I COULDN'T THINK WHERE **ELSE** TO TURN."

"THE **HOUSE** WAS STILL THERE...

BUT THE PEOPLE WHO LIVED THERE SAID THEY'D BOUGHT IT IN AUCTION TEN YEARS AGO. THEY SAID THE PREVIOUS OWNERS HAD **DIED** JUST BEFORE THAT..."

"I MUST HAVE TURNED ASHEN, BECAUSE THEY ASKED ME IF I WAS ALL RIGHT, AND OFFERED ME A CUP OF TEA. THEY SEEMED LIKE NICE PEOPLE...

BUT I WAS SO UPSET I PRACTICALLY **RAN** AWAY DOWN THE STREET..."

"THEN I SAW A TELEPHONE — NOT IN A BOX, JUST ON A POLE THING — AND THOUGHT OF CALLING *JOCELYN*...

THE TELEPHONE WOULDN'T TAKE MY MONEY EITHER, BUT I MANAGED TO GET HOLD OF THE OPERATOR..."

COULD YOU CONNECT ME WITH LEWES 459, PLEASE — AND REVERSE THE CHARGES.

YOU WANT 01273 459, CALLER?

I'M SORRY, CALLER — THAT NUMBER IS INCOMPLETE...

IT IS?

ER... DO I?

"SHE PUT ME THROUGH TO DIRECTORY OF ENQUIRIES, AND I ASKED THEM TO GIVE ME THE *RIGHT* NUMBER FOR JOCELYN'S PARENTS.

THEY *COULDN'T*. THERE WAS NO ENTRY FOR THEM IN THE DIRECTORY AT ALL."

"SO I ASKED THEM TO CHECK *OTHER* NUMBERS — ALL THE FRIENDS I COULD THINK OF, EVEN MY BOSS...

BUT THEY COULDN'T FIND *ANY* OF THEM. EVEN THE ARCHITECTURAL FIRM I WORKED FOR DIDN'T EXIST ANYMORE...

AND AFTER THE FOURTH NAME CAME UP BLANK, THEY TOLD ME TO STOP WASTING THEIR TIME AND HUNG UP ON ME.

AND THEN IT STARTED TO RAIN...

AND I FELT SOMETHING *SNAP* INSIDE ME."

128

129

"I DIDN'T KNOW WHAT TO DO, OR WHERE TO GO. I WENT TO A HOSPITAL, BUT THEY WOULDN'T LISTEN. SAID I HAD TO WAIT MY TURN, AND THERE WERE HUNDREDS OF PEOPLE IN FRONT OF ME. SOME OF THEM WERE SHOUTING AND SWEARING ... IT WAS HORRIBLE. I WAITED TILL I JUST COULDN'T STAND IT ANYMORE, THEN I LEFT..."

"I WANDERED. I DON'T KNOW WHERE. SLEPT WHERE AND WHEN I COULD, IN DOORWAYS, IN THE PARK.

"THE POLICE KEPT WAKING ME UP AND MOVING ME ON."

"THEY DIDN'T WANT TO LISTEN TO MY STORY EITHER.

IT WAS HOT, AND THEN IT WAS RAINING, AND THEN IT WAS HOT AGAIN."

"SOMETIMES IT WAS DARK, SOMETIMES I ATE AT A SOUP KITCHEN VAN-THING I'D STUMBLED ACROSS..."

"AND I TRIED TO REMEMBER ALL THE BAD THINGS I'D DONE IN MY LIFE, TO BE PUNISHED THIS WAY.

BECAUSE I KNEW WHERE I WAS NOW...

"I WAS IN HELL."

BOSTON, MASS.—
JUNE 28th. 1996.

TEA, MISS SMITH?

BARMENO & ROCKWELL

ATTORNEYS AT LAW

WOT, PROPER TEA?

THASS VERY CIVIL OF YOU—I DON' MIN' IF I DO.

TEA FOR TWO, PLEASE, MISS MAYTHORPE.

IS THERE SOME SORTER PROBLEM WIV GETTIN' ME STUFF? ONLY YORE YOUNG MAN'S BIN GONE FER AGES...

I'M AFRAID HE'S HAD TO GO DOWN TO OUR VAULTS IN THE BASEMENT.

HE SHOULDN'T BE MUCH LONGER.

YOU KNOW, YOU'VE TAKEN US RATHER BY SURPRISE. YOU'RE THE FIRST MEMBER OF YOUR FAMILY TO ACTUALLY VISIT OUR OFFICES IN NEARLY TWO HUNDRED YEARS...

YOU DON' SAY?

WELL, YOU KNOW HOW IT IS—WOT WIV ONE FING AND ANUVVER, I BIN A BIT BUSY.

AH, HERE HE IS... AND THE TEA.

YOU KNOW, IT MAY BE MORE ECONOMICAL TO TRANSFER THE CARE OF THIS TO A BANK...

NAH. I DON' TRUST THER BUGGERS. NEVER 'AVE DONE, NEVER WILL.

NOW THEN...

LESS JUS' SEE WOT THAT NICE MR. JEFFERSON LEFT US.

TO BE CONTINUED

the DREAMING

THE NEXT DAY...

THE LOST BOY

Part Three

Peter Hogan • Writer
Steve Parkhouse • Artist
Daniel Vozzo • Colors&Seps

Alisa Kwitney • Editor
Neil Gaiman • Consultant

The Dreaming created by Neil Gaiman

YES?

MRS. HARRIS?

YES?

MRS. JOCELYN HARRIS? MISS GREENFORD AS WAS?

THIS IS ABOUT BRIAN, ISN'T IT? NOBODY EVER CALLS ME THAT UNLESS IT'S TO DO WITH HIM...

YOU'D BETTER COME IN.

SO WHICH ARE YOU? A REPORTER, OR ONE OF THE U.F.O. BRIGADE?

er, NEITHER, ACTUALLY. I'M A UNIVERSITY PROFESSOR — MY NAME IS JENKINS...

I'M WRITING A PAPER ON HOW THE MEDIA REPORTS MISSING PERSONS, AND I JUST GOT... INTERESTED IN BRIAN'S CASE. I WAS HOPING TO ASK YOU A FEW QUESTIONS...

WHY NOT? AT LEAST IT MAKES A CHANGE FROM THE SAUCER-SPOTTERS —

I'M HEARTILY SICK OF THEM.

THEY THINK BRIAN WAS AN EARLY VICTIM OF ALIEN ABDUCTION.

TEA?

YES, THANK YOU...

IT SEEMS A FEW PEOPLE SAW STRANGE LIGHTS IN THE SKY OVER ASHDOWN FOREST, THE SAME NIGHT THAT BRIAN VANISHED...

ONE OF THESE CHAPS WROTE A BOOK ABOUT IT, ABOUT TWENTY YEARS AGO, AND I'VE HAD A STEADY TRICKLE OF FANATICS TURNING UP AT MY DOOR EVER SINCE...

NO OFFENSE.

NONE TAKEN. IT'S VERY GOOD OF YOU TO SPARE ME THE TIME.

OH, I'VE GOT PLENTY OF THAT, NOW THE KIDS HAVE ALL FLOWN THE COOP...

ODDLY ENOUGH, BRIAN WAS INTERESTED IN ALL THAT SAUCER NONSENSE HIMSELF, I USED TO TEASE HIM ABOUT IT... AND NOW IT'S MADE HIM FAMOUS, SORT OF.

NO. *I* THINK BRIAN MUST HAVE BEEN *MURDERED.*

AT LEAST THAT WOULD EXPLAIN WHY THEY NEVER FOUND A BODY— THE MURDERER MIGHT HAVE HIDDEN IT.

WHAT MAKES YOU THINK THAT? DID BRIAN HAVE ANY ENEMIES?

NO, OF *COURSE* NOT. BUT PERHAPS HE PICKED UP A HITCHHIKER WHO JUST HAPPENED TO BE A HOMICIDAL MANIAC. IT *DOES* HAPPEN.

AND IT'S AN ODD PART OF THE COUNTRY, ROUND THERE.

YES...

BUT I STILL FELT I'D BEEN DESERTED, SOMEHOW. I SUPPOSE IT WAS THE FIRST TIME I'D REALLY HAD TO *DEAL* WITH DEATH.... AND I THINK THEIR NOT FINDING A BODY JUST MADE IT ALL THE MORE GRISLY...

ANYWAY, LIFE WENT ON. A YEAR LATER TOM AND I ANNOUNCED OUR ENGAGEMENT, AND LIVED HAPPILY EVER AFTER.

I KNOW IT SOUNDS TERRIBLE, BUT I HARDLY EVER GAVE POOR BRIAN A THOUGHT UNTIL THE SAUCER BUSINESS STARTED....

IS THIS YOUR FAMILY?

YES, THAT'S THEM. THE YOUNGEST IS AT OXFORD NOW, DOING HER PhD....

TEMPUS FUGIT AND ALL THAT, EH?

139

AND SOME OF IT'S INCOMPREHENSIBLE.

I MEAN, I CAN'T MAKE HEAD OR TAIL OF THOSE *HIPPIE* CHAPS...

OH, I DON'T KNOW.

I ALWAYS THOUGHT THEY WERE RATHER FUN...

WHAT ABOUT... YOU KNOW, ME? ANY LUCK?

EH?

WELL, THOSE X-RAYS SHOWED I WAS ALL RIGHT, SO... YOU *HAVE* BEEN CHECKING MY STORY, HAVEN'T YOU?

YES. YES, I HAVE. AND I DON'T KNOW IF LUCK IS *QUITE* THE RIGHT WORD, BUT...

YES, I HAVE.

Architect feared dead

London man missing for a week

POLICE are expressing fears for the safety of architect Brian Salmon, London home for over e not ruled out the play after a car was at the edge of the n Forest.

said last night they to the public for any e whereabouts

Hopes fade for Brian Salmon

Speaking from his London home last night, Bill Salmon, father of missing architect Brian Salmon, said the

HAVE YOU SEEN THIS MAN?

With compliments

Ted

I BELIEVE YOU, BRIAN.

I CAN'T *BEGIN* TO UNDERSTAND *HOW* THIS HAS HAPPENED, BUT I'VE SEEN ENOUGH TO CONVINCE *ANYBODY*. I *DO* BELIEVE YOU.

SO... ER, WHAT DO WE DO NOW?

FRANKLY, I HAVE **NO** IDEA.

WASHINGTON, D.C. JULY 4th. 1996.

GOOD **EVENIN!** MISTER PRESIDENT.

AN' A VERY 'APPY **HINDEPENDENCE** DAY TO YER.

Heh.

THASS NOT A BAD LIKENESS. YOU ALWAYS WOZ A **GOOD-LOOKIN'** OLE BUGGER.

OH, I KNOWS YOU AIN'T 'ERE. THEY TELLS ME YER BURIED DOWN IN VIRGINYER.

BUT I AIN'T GOT TIME TER GO TRAIPSIN' ALL THER WAY DOWN THERE. I'M RUSHED OFF ME FEET AS IT IS.

BLEEDIN' FINGS IS GIVIN' ME GYP, AN' ALL.

ANYWAY, I RECKONS YER CAN 'EAR ME WELL ENOUGH.

SEE, IT TOOK A WHILE, BUT I FINALLY GOT 'OLD OF THER WOSSNAME.

AN' IT'S ALL BIN A BIT OF A PIG'S BREAKFAS', WOT WIV ONE FING AN' ANUVVER, BUT NEVER MIND, EH?

I GOT 'ERE ON TIME, AN' THASS THER MAIN FING.

"HIN THE NATION'S CAPITAL," AN' TWO HUNDRID AN' TWENNY YEARS TER THE DAY SINCE YOU GOT GIVEN IT.

JUS' LIKE YOU ARRANGED.

OH, ISS YOU. IS IT?

I MIGHTER *KNOWN* IT'D BE WUNNER *YOU* LOT.

I HAVE COME FOR...

YES, YES, *I* KNOWS. I 'EARD THE 'OLE STORY FROM MISTER J. 'ISSELF.

OF 'OW 'IM AN' JOHN ADAMS AN' MISTER FRANKLIN WOZ TRYIN' TER DESIGN A *GREAT SEAL* FER THER NEW NATION...

AN' 'OW NUFFING THEY CAME UP WIV WOZ ANY GOOD...

"SO MISTER J., 'E GOES OFF FER A WALK IN THER GARDIN, TER CLEAR 'IS 'EAD. AN' 'OO SHOULD 'E MEET BUT A *TALL STRANGER*, WEARIN' A BIG CLOAK WOT 'IDES 'IS FACE. AN' THER STRANGER SEZ..."

BE NOT AFRAID.

THIS WILL SERVE YOUR PURPOSE.

"SO MISTER J., 'E RUSHES IN TER SHOW THE UVVERS. AN' WHEN THEY SEES WOT THEY **GOT**, THEY ALL RUSHES BACK OUT AGAIN, TER FANK THER STRANGER..."

"BUT 'E WOZ GORN— VANISHED INTO FIN AIR."

NOT VERY **PERLITE**, ARE YER? YOU **SHY** OR **SUMMINK**?

THEIR NEED—AND THE LAND'S— WAS ANSWERED.

TARRYING WOULD HAVE SERVED NO PURPOSE.

BUT HE AND I **DID** MEET ONCE AGAIN, DURING HIS PRESIDENCY. AT THAT TIME WE ARRANGED THIS APPOINTMENT, AND '''OTHER THINGS.

YOU HAVE THE SCROLL?

ISS **MORE** THAN JUST A DRAWIN', AIN' IT?

MUCH MORE. BUT NOW ITS DAY IS DONE.

FIRSTBORN? ATTEND US...

149

WHAT AM I GOING TO **DO**, MURIEL?

WELL.... I HAD A CHAT WITH A PRIVATE DETECTIVE FRIEND OF MINE.

HE CAN EASILY GET YOU A NEW PASSPORT AND EMPLOYMENT PAPERS— **FORGED**, OF COURSE...

BUT THE PRICE SEEMED VERY REASONABLE.

BUT.... EVEN IF I **COULD** START A NEW LIFE HERE, THIS ISN'T **MY** WORLD. I'LL NEVER **BELONG**. I'M ALWAYS GOING TO FEEL LIKE AN EXILE...

OR SOME KIND OF... LIVING **FOSSIL**...

THANKS. I'M **YOUNGER** THAN YOU, REMEMBER?

YES. BUT IT'S ALL RIGHT FOR YOU. **YOU** GOT HERE ONE DAY AT A TIME. YOU SAW IT ALL HAPPEN, SLOWLY. HAVING TO TAKE THIS ALL IN AT **ONCE**...

IT'S... TOO MUCH FOR ME.

THOUGH... I CAN SEE THAT IT'S AS GOOD AS IT'S BAD. I MEAN, COMPUTERS ARE **AMAZING**, AND VIDEOS...

AND THE **FOOD** IS **SMASHING**.

I'D NEVER **HAD** CHINESE FOOD UNTIL THE OTHER NIGHT. OR PIZZA. OR **CURRY**...

MY TASTEBUDS HAVE NEVER **HAD** IT SO GOOD.

BUT YOU'RE RIGHT— I **AM** HOMESICK. I MISS MY FAMILY...

AND THE WORLD I KNEW. IT MIGHT HAVE BEEN A BIT DULL...

BUT AT LEAST I **UNDERSTOOD** IT.

YOU KNOW, SOME PHYSICISTS BELIEVE THAT THE PRESENT *ISN'T* JUST THE CULMINATION OF PAST EVENTS. THEY THINK THAT THE *FUTURE* MIGHT ALSO HAVE A HAND IN SHAPING IT SOMEHOW...

OF COURSE, THEN THEY DRAG IN *PARALLEL UNIVERSES*, AND IT ALL GETS A BIT MIND-BOGGLING.

SORRY —YOU'VE LOST ME...

DON'T YOU SEE? IF THE FUTURE *DOES* HELP CREATE THE PRESENT...

THEN PERHAPS WHAT WE CAN DO *NOW* CAN CHANGE THE *PAST*. AND PERHAPS YOU *CAN* GET BACK HOME.

NO, I CAN'T.

I MEAN, WE *KNOW* I CAN'T GET BACK. I'M OFFICIALLY *DEAD*, FOR GOD'S SAKE. FANCY THEORIES WON'T CHANGE *THAT*.

NO. BUT SOMETHING ELSE MIGHT.

MAGIC.

IT'S BEEN KNOCKING AT MY DOOR ALL MY LIFE, AND I'VE JUST... PRETENDED IT WASN'T THERE.

AND NOW I ...CAN'T *DENY* IT ANYMORE.

DID I EVER TELL YOU ABOUT HOW I MET HETTIE?

THE OLD WOMAN WHO FOUND ME? NO...

AND.... THOUGH I **STILL** DON'T QUITE UNDERSTAND **HOW**, WE BECAME FRIENDS, AFTER A FASHION.

SHE TEACHES ME A LITTLE – A **VERY** LITTLE, I SUSPECT – OF WHAT SHE KNOWS. AND IN RETURN, I DO THE ODD ERRAND FOR HER.

LIKE?

OH, SHOPPING, MAINLY. SHE HAS A FONDNESS FOR **CHOCOLATE ANTS**, AND FORTNUMS WON'T LET HER IN ANYMORE.

NOT AFTER THE **LAST** TIME.

SHE **CLAIMS** TO BE OVER TWO HUNDRED AND FIFTY YEARS OLD. AND I **USED** TO THINK SHE WAS LYING. UNTIL NOW....

I'M NOT SO SURE. I THINK SHE CAN **HELP** YOU, BRIAN. SHE'S BEEN MIXED UP IN THIS FROM THE START, AND SHE **KNOWS** THINGS.

SUCH AS?

SUCH AS 'OW TER FIND PEOPLE WOT'S **LOST**, FER A START.

HETTIE.... THANK **GOODNESS** YOU'RE BACK.

THIS.... IS HETTIE?

THEN.... I WANT TO GO **HOME**, DEFINITELY.

IS THERE A **PROBLEM**, HETTIE? YOU CAN **DO** IT, CAN'T YOU?

I GAVE THER BOY MY **WORD**, DIDDEN I? I'LL GET 'IM THERE **SOME'OW**.

BUGGER. OH, WELL, IT WAS WORF A TRY....

THAT SOUNDS AS IF THERE **ARE** PROBLEMS.

HO, YES, DEARY — I FINK YOU COULD SAY **THAT** ALL RIGHT.

SEE, WE'RE GONNER 'AVE TER DEAL WIV THER **GENTRY**.

YOU KNOW.... THER **FAIR FOLK**.

AN' THASS ABOUT AS **PROBLEMATICK** AS FINGS CAN **GET**.

HOW STRANGE. I DIDN'T EVEN BAT AN EYELID AT THAT. APPARENTLY NOW I EVEN BELIEVE IN FAIRIES.

'COURSE YOU DOES.

ONLY YOU SHOULDEN CALL 'EM THAT. ISS **DISRESPECKFUL**.

NOT TER MENTION DOWNRIGHT BLEEDIN' **DANGEROUS**.

Next
THE
WILD
WOOD

BUGGERED IF *I* KNOW, DEAR.

STILL, ISS WORF A *TRY*, INNIT?

HERE IT IS...

ROAD ATLAS

RIGHT, I'LL MEET YOU *'ERE*, AT TWILIGHT ON THER FIFTEENTH.

RIGHT...

THASS *SETTLED* THEN.

HETTIE? WHERE ARE YOU *GOING*?

I 'AVE GOT *UVVER* FINGS TER DO, Y'KNOW.

SEE YER NEX' WEEK. NIGHTY *NIGHT*.

tch. SOME PEOPLE FINKS THEY *OWNS* YER.

THE ASHDOWN FOREST, JULY 15TH, 1996.

THIS IS THE PLACE...

THE LOST BOY

Part Four

Peter Hogan • Writer
Steve Parkhouse • Penciller
Dick Giordano • Inker
Annie Parkhouse • Letterer
Daniel Vozzo • Colors&Seps

Alisa Kwitney • Editor
Neil Gaiman • Consultant

The Dreaming created by Neil Gaiman

ANY SIGN OF HETTIE?

NO— CAN'T SEE HER.

WELL, DON'T WORRY—I DON'T SUPPOSE SHE'LL BE LONG.

SO...THIS IS IT.

YES... I SUPPOSE SO.

WELL, HERE'S TEN POUNDS IN OLD MONEY, AND TWENTY IN NEW. JUST IN CASE.

MURIEL, YOU *SHOULDN'T.* YOU'VE DONE *MORE* THAN ENOUGH FOR ME ALREADY...

163

NONSENSE. I COULDN'T BEAR TO THINK OF YOU *STRANDED* SOMEWHERE, FOR WANT OF A FEW POUNDS.

AND I'VE MADE YOU SOME SANDWICHES, AND A THERMOS, AND THERE'S A TORCH IN HERE, AND SOME BISCUITS...

I SHALL *MISS* YOU, YOU KNOW.

IT'S BEEN... *NICE*, HAVING SOMEONE TO TALK TO IN THE EVENINGS...

YOU *READY* THEN?

ONLY I DON' WANNER 'ANG ABOUT 'ERE ALL NIGHT.

I CAN'T COME WITH YOU, CAN I? NOT EVEN PART-WAY?

NO. DEARY. 'FRAID NOT.

BUT YOU *WILL* LET ME KNOW WHAT HAPPENS. *WON'T* YOU, HETTIE?

'COURSE.

RIGHT, BONNIE BOY— WE BES' BE MAKIN' A *MOVE*...

LOOK, DON' GET BLEEDIN' *FILLERSOFFICLE* ON ME—I GOT *ENUFF* PROBLEMS. AN' GET THAT *LIGHT* OUTTER ME FACE.

YER ALL *RIGHT,* IN'CHER?

YES, I'M...

APPROACH US, CHILD.

WE MEAN YOU NO HARM.

WE HAVE *HEARD* YOUR TALE, BRIAN SALMON. WHAT IS IT THAT YOU WISH OF US?

PLEASE, UM, YOUR MAJESTY...

I JUST WANT TO GO *HOME.*

TO DENY YOU WOULD BE A *CRUEL* THING... AND WE WOULD *NOT* HAVE YOUR COMPANION THINK *ILL* OF US...

Hmph.

AND SO... WE *GRANT* YOUR PASSAGE. FARE YOU *WELL,* MORTAL.

WOMAN, DO NOT *FORGET*— IN RETURN FOR OUR GOOD WILL IN THIS MATTER, YOU WILL BRING TO US THE ITEM OF WHICH WE SPOKE, OR *ELSE*...

I *SWORE,* DIDDEN I?

THAT YOU DID. UNTIL *THEN,* THEN.

HETTIE? *WHAT* DID YOU SWEAR?

YOU MIND YER *OWN.* IT AIN' A PARTER *YORE* STORY.

PORT AN' LEMON AN' A PINTA BITTER, PLEASE, LUV.

AN' ANY CHANCE YOU GOT SOME LETTIS FER MY RABBIT?

I'LL SEE WHAT I CAN DO.

THIS ONE'S ON *YOU*, BONNIE BOY.

GIVE THER GENNELMAN BE'IND THER BAR YORE *BAG*, AN' THAT *TWENNY QUID* MURIEL GAVE YER. THEY DON' *BELONG* IN YORE WORLD.

IF YOU SAY SO...

GOOD LAD.

NOW, LESS GO AN' GRAB A SEAT BY THER WINDER.

SEE, THIS IS WOSS CALLED A *FREE 'OUSE*...

IS THAT REALLY... *WATER* OUT THERE?

172

IT LOOKS LIKE...WE'RE *SAILING*.

THAT WE ARE, BONNIE BOY. BUT THASS NOT WATER— THASS *TIME*.

AS I WOZ SAYIN', THIS *AIN'* JUS' A PUB—ISS ALSO WOTCHER MIGHT CALL A *MODER TRANSPORT*.

LOOK, I KNOW I'M *NEVER* GOING TO UNDERSTAND *ALL* OF THIS, BUT CAN I ASK...

WHY DID YOU PICK *ME*?

I NEVER PICKED YER, BONNIE BOY. YOU PICKED *YERSELF*.

I JUS' USED YER 'CAUSE YOU WOZ *THERE*, ALL 'ANDY-LIKE. AN' I *NEEDED* YORE 'ELP, TER KEEP THAT KEY...

OUT OF THE HANDS OF YOUR ENEMY. AND WHAT HAPPENED TO HIM?

HENEMY? PR'APS SHE *WOZ*, AT THAT...THOUGH I SEEMS TER RECALL A TIME WHEN WE WOZ FRIENDS.

DEAD NOW, O' COURSE. *YEARS* AGO.

NATCHERAL CAUSES, BEFORE YOU ARSKS.

WYCH CROSS, 25TH OCTOBER, 1859.

Wha?

FEELING *BETTER*, MILADY? HAD A NICE LITTLE *NAP*, HAVE WE?

I WAS MERELY RESTING MY EYES...

AND I STILL HAVE *ALL* MY WITS, GIRL. TREAT ME LIKE A CHILD, AND I SHALL *BEHAVE* LIKE ONE.

WHERE ARE YOU TAKING ME?

TO YOUR *BIRTHDAY BANQUET*, MILADY.

IMAGINE— YOU'RE *NINETY-NINE* TODAY...

DAM' YER IMPUDENCE, GIRL— I *KNOW* HOW OLD I AM.

SO...SHE KEPT FAITH WITH ME.

WHO DID, MILADY?

174

NO ONE.

STOP HERE— I WISH TO VIEW THE SUNSET FOR A WHILE.

RAKES AND WASTERS, THE PACK OF 'EM—TO THE DEVIL WITH 'EM ALL.

BUT... MILADY... YOUR FAMILY IS WAITING FOR US DOWNSTAIRS.

IF YOU SAY SO, MILADY.

LISTEN... CAN YOU HEAR?

HEAR WHAT, MILADY?

HE IS SINGING...

SUCH... BEAUTY...

I BELIEVE... IT IS TIME...

NO, MILADY! YOU'VE NOT TO EXERT YOUR—

MILADY!

175

177

'ERE, CLERISSA'S SCRATCHIN' AT THER DOOR.

I FINK THIS MUS' BE YORE STOP.

IT'S MORNING...

YEAH, THIS LOOKS FERMILIAR...

I RECKON YER CAR'S DOWN THAT WAY.

HETTIE...

NAH—DON' TRY AN' SAY NUFFINK FLOW'RY. WE'RE QUITS NOW, YOU AN' ME.

UM, WILL YOU DO SOMETHING FOR ME?

KEEP AN EYE ON MURIEL? MAKE SURE SHE LOOKS AFTER HERSELF?

'COURSE.

THEN... I SUPPOSE THIS IS GOODBYE.

MIND 'OW YER GO, THEN.

"KEEP AN EYE ON MURIEL"... HMPH.

AS IF I AIN'T BIN DOIN' THAT FER YEARS.

ARE YOU ALL RIGHT?

YES... I THINK SO. JUST GRAZED MY HAND A BIT...

AT LEAST THE RABBIT GOT AWAY. I THINK MY BIKE'S FARED WORSE THAN I HAVE...

IT'S NOT TOO BAD. THE CHAIN'S COME OFF, THAT'S ALL.

SOON HAVE THAT FIXED FOR YOU...

♪♫

YOU SOUND CHEERFUL.

DO I?

WELL, THE SUN'S SHINING, AND THE BIRDS ARE SINGING, AND...

IT'S GOOD TO BE HOME.

OH, HAVE YOU BEEN AWAY SOMEWHERE?

YES, YOU MIGHT SAY THAT.

THERE. THAT SHOULD HOLD YOU FOR A WHILE.

THE END.

HIS BROTHER'S KEEPER

The Dreaming

"His Brother's Keeper"

Number 8

by
Alisa Kwitney
and
Michael Zulli

IMAGINE A STORY THAT BEGINS LIKE THIS: ONCE UPON A TIME OUTSIDE OF TIME THERE IS A PLACE THAT IS NOT A PLACE.

THEN YOU FORGET IT IS A DREAM. YOU FORGET THAT YOU ARE IN IT.

IT FEELS SO FAMILIAR AND SO STRANGE THAT YOU RECOGNIZE IT AS A DREAM.

AND NOW YOU CAN SEE TWO HOUSES STANDING CLOSE TOGETHER, DIVIDED BY A GRAVEYARD.

ONE CONTAINS MYSTERIES, THE OTHER SECRETS. BUT WHICH IS WHICH? IN DREAMS NO ANSWER IS OBVIOUS.

YOU CHOOSE THE ONE ON THE RIGHT.

AND THEN YOU ARE INSIDE A DREAM SO OLD YOU KNOW IT COULDN'T POSSIBLY BELONG JUST TO YOU.

AND EVEN THOUGH THE PEOPLE IN THIS DREAM ARE LOOKING IN YOUR DIRECTION, YOU FEEL THAT THEIR ATTENTION IS FOCUSED ON SOMEONE JUST BEHIND YOU.

HE SMELLS OF THE OUTSIDE, OF WOODSMOKE AND RESIN, AND ALTHOUGH HE DOESN'T ACKNOWLEDGE YOUR PRESENCE, YOU SENSE THAT *HE* CAN SEE YOU--

--EVEN IF THE OTHERS *CANNOT*.

HIS BROTHER'S KEEPER

ALISA KWITNEY — MICHAEL ZULLI — DANIEL VOZZO — TODD KLEIN —
WRITER — ARTIST — COLORIST / SEPS — LETTERER —
KAREN BERGER, EDITOR • THE DREAMING CREATED BY NEIL GAIMAN

TWO MORE GUESTS ARRIVE IN TIME FOR DINNER. THE FIRST, A TALL, THIN GENTLEMAN SAYS, IN A 1940'S *BBC* ACCENT, THAT HIS NAME IS LUCIEN.

THE SECOND, A FAT MAN IN A FEZ, SPOTS SETH IN A CORNER AND GASPS AS IF HE'D SEEN A GHOST. HE THEN CONSOLES HIMSELF WITH A LARGE PLATE OF OLIVES AND CHEESE.

I DON'T GET IT, LUCIEN. IF HE HATES HIS BROTHER, THEN WHY INVITE HIM TO STAY FOR DINNER?

IF HOSTILITY KEPT FAMILIES FROM EATING TO-GETHER, THE WHOLE WORLD WOULD STARVE.

ACTUALLY, CAIN IS FOLLOWING AN OLD CUSTOM. ONCE YOU CROSS A PERSON'S THRESHOLD, YOU ARE CONSIDERED A GUEST, AND AS SUCH MUST BE FED AND SHELTERED, AND IN NO WISE HARMED.

SA-SA-SO, SE-SE-SETH, WHA-WHA-WHAT--

YES, WHAT *DOES* BRING YOU HERE, SETH? NEED A SPARE KIDNEY, OR SIMPLY OVERCOME BY NOSTALGIA?

I BELIEVE ABEL WAS ASKING THE QUESTION, CAIN. WHAT WAS IT, ABEL?

OH. I WA-WAS JUST CU-CURIOUS AB-ABOUT--

WEH-WEH-WE HA-HAVEN'T BEEN CLOSE, REALLY. YA-YOU WE-WERE SO MUCH YOUNGER THAN--I MU-MEAN, YOU WE-WERE BORN AFTER--

DON'T I KNOW IT. EVER SINCE I WAS A KID, I'VE FELT LIKE I'VE COME IN ON THE MIDDLE OF THE MOVIE. IT'S LIKE, I'M TRYING TO FIGURE OUT WHO I AM, BUT PART OF THE PUZZLE'S MISSING.

IT'S BEEN LONELY, BEING THE YOUNGEST. I NEVER REALLY FELT LIKE I HAD BROTHERS. I THOUGHT IT WAS TIME FOR ME TO GET TO KNOW YOU.

LEARN THE FAMILY SECRETS.

ZIFT. DREK. BULLSHIT.

EXCUSE ME, BUT DON'T YOU THINK YOUR BROTHERS SHOULD HAVE COME BACK BY NOW?

SH-SH-SHOULD THEY?

ASK HIM HOW MANY *PEAS* ARE ON HIS PLATE. I BET HE'D KNOW THE ANSWER TO *THAT*.

WUH-WELL, I'LL JU-JUST HAVE TO GUH-GUH-GUH-GO GET THEM, RU-RU-RIGHT AFTER I FI-FINISH THIS DI-DI-DISH.

ABEL.

I THINK THERE'S SOMETHING YOU SHOULD SEE.

EVE?

WUH-WUH-WHAT...

NOW, ABEL.

196

FEELING BETTER, SETH?

NOT REALLY, I SEE. PERHAPS YOU'RE ALLERGIC TO MANDRAKE ROOT. OH, WELL.

THEN AGAIN, YOU MIGHT BE DYING. MAYBE I'VE KILLED YOU. THAT'S A MYSTERY, ISN'T IT? WHY FAMILY MEMBERS *MURDER* EACH OTHER.

DON'T YOU WONDER WHAT ADAM THOUGHT WHEN HE SAW HIS WIFE DELIVER A LITTLE SCRAP OF SQUALLING FLESH? FOR ALL HE KNEW I WAS A NOISY TUMOR, OR A DEMON OR SOMETHING.

AND WHAT ABOUT MY MOTHER? DID SHE CONSIDER MURDER AS I WENT THROUGH THE TERRIBLE TWOS? IS THAT WHY SHE NAMED HER SECOND SON ABEL, FOR "GRIEF"?

WHY DON'T MORE MOTHERS KILL THEIR KIDS?

YOU SEE, SETH, IT'S JUST AS MR. FREUD SUSPECT- ED. FRATRICIDE AND INCEST, A PART OF EVERY FAMILY'S MAKEUP.

CAIN!

HAVE YOU MURDERED *THIS* BROTHER, TOO?

NO, HE'S JUST EATEN SOMETHING THAT'S DISAGREED WITH HIM.

CU-CU-CAIN, SHU-SHE'S GONE.

SHE'D GONE INSANE, ABEL. SHE WASN'T THE SISTER YOU REMEMBERED. SHE'D SIT NAKED ON THE ROOF AND CUT HERSELF. SHE SMEARED... WASTE MATTER ON THE WALLS OF THE RED ROOM.

I THOUGHT IT KINDER TO KEEP HER THAN SEND HER AWAY.

LIAR!

I WASN'T INSANE. I WAS HURTING. WHEN WOMEN FEEL TOO MUCH PAIN, MEN ALWAYS SAY THEY'RE ACTING CRAZY.

BUT HOW WOULD YOU LIKE IT, KNOWING YOU WERE SO-- SO HORRIBLE AND FAT THAT A MAN WOULD KILL RATHER THAN HAVE YOU?

MEL, I--

AND YOU WANTED HER, TOO! I SAW YOU WITH HER NIGHTGOWN, STUFFING IT UNDER YOUR PILLOW WHERE YOU COULD SMELL IT EVERY NIGHT!

YOU HAVE TO BE DESIR-ABLE, TO MAKE IT INTO THE BOOK. YOU HAVE TO BE PRETTY ENOUGH TO WORK SEVEN YEARS FOR, OR ELSE HISTORY FORGETS YOU.

MEN MUST BE HOLY, YOU SEE, BUT WOMEN SHOULD HAVE A MORE EARTHY APPEAL. LIKE SARAH. AND RACHEL. LIKE REBECCA AND RUTH AND ESTHER. THE BIBLE SAYS IT: BEAUTIES, ALL.

LEAH WAS PLAIN, OF COURSE, BUT SHE HAD TO HIDE HER UGLY FACE UNDER A HEAVY VEIL, TO FOOL HER SISTER'S MAN INTO FUCKING HER.

DOES THAT SHOCK YOU? BUT I BET YOU WANT TO FUCK MY SISTER. MEN ALWAYS DO. THEY WANT TO RESCUE ACLIMA, AND THEN THEY WANT THEIR REWARD.

DOES SHE NEED RESCUING?

OF COURSE SHE DOES. AND WHILE YOU CARRY HER TO SAFETY, SHE'LL SINK HER CLAWS RIGHT IN YOU, AND BY THE TIME YOU FEEL IT...YOU'LL BE SCARRED.

BUT WHAT DOES SHE NEED RESCUING FROM? IS SHE IN DANGER?

JUST SHUT UP ABOUT HER!

SWAK!

NOW IF YOU DON'T MIND, I WANT TO GO BACK TO MY *HOUSE*.

IT'S NOT *YOUR* HOUSE, YOU DEMENTED TROLLOP. FEEL FREE TO REMAIN UP IN YOUR DINGY ATTIC, BUT VENTURE DOWNSTAIRS AND I'LL MAKE YOU SORRY YOU WERE EVER BORN.

I'M NOT AFRAID OF YOU ANYMORE, CAIN. AND I'LL COME DOWN WHEN-EVER I WANT TO.

WHENEVER I WANT TO.

I THINK IT'S TIME WE LEFT, MATTHEW.

DO WE HAVE TO? I WANT TO SEE THIS OUT TO THE END.

YOU'RE ALL OLD ENOUGH TO MAKE YOUR OWN MIS-TAKES.

BUT I'M TOO OLD TO WATCH YOU MAKE THEM.

JUMELLA SAID HER SISTER NEEDED RESCUING. WHAT HAPPENED TO ACLIMA? *WHERE* IS SHE NOW?

WHERE NO MAN WILL LAY HIS GREASY, SWEATY PAWS ON HER, LEAST OF ALL *YOU*, YOU CRINGING PUP.

WHO ARE YOU PROTECTING, CAIN? YOUR *SISTER*? OR *YOURSELF*?

BUT I FORGOT, YOU'RE ALREADY PROTECTED WITH GOD'S MARK. *NO ONE* CAN HARM YOU, CAN THEY?

OR AT LEAST, NO ONE IN THEIR *RIGHT MIND* WOULD TRY.

AND WHILE YOU PONDER THAT, PONDER THIS: I'M GOING TO *FIND* ACLIMA, CAIN, WHETHER YOU *HELP* ME OR NOT.

GOOD LUCK, THEN, BABY BROTHER. YOU'RE GOING TO NEED IT WHEN YOU MEET *MY TWIN*.

GODSPEED HIM IF HE CAN HELP YOU, MY SISTER, FOR GOD KNOWS THAT I CANNOT.

205

SUDDENLY THE DREAM SHIFTS FOCUS, AS DREAMS SOMETIMES DO. YOU HOVER SOMEWHERE ABOVE THE ACTION AS CAIN APOLOGIZES TO DANA AND ZOE.

NO ONE APOLOGIZES TO YOU.

THE DREAM IS ENDING WITHOUT RESOLVING ALL ITS MYSTERIES, AND YOU FEEL A LITTLE CHEATED. WHAT HAPPENED TO BYRON? WHERE DID SETH GO?

BUT SOME STORIES END IN THE MIDDLE, WITHOUT RESOLUTION.

A YOUNG GIRL NAMED ZOE LEVINE DISAPPEARS ON A ROAD TO EILAT, LEAVING BEHIND A BOOK OF POEMS, A PAIR OF SANDALS, A HEBREW DICTIONARY, AND A MARTIN GUITAR, WHICH ARE SENT BACK TO GRIEVING PARENTS IN UPSTATE NEW YORK.

A WRY FORTY-FIVE-YEAR-OLD ACCOUNTANT NAMED DANA CLEVELAND DIES AS THE FIRST NEW BUDS OF APRIL APPEAR, AND THE AUTOPSY REVEALS NO APPARENT CAUSE.

IN HIS LIBRARY, LUCIEN NOTICES THAT DANA WROTE THREE WELL-RECEIVED MYSTERY NOVELS UNDER THE PEN NAME OF BYRON MANNING.

MYSTERY AND SECRETS, THE CLOSEST OF SIBLINGS. YOU BEGIN WALKING TOWARD THE HOUSE ON THE LEFT.

THE END.